Mesopotamia

Julian Reade

Published for The Trustees of The British Museum by BRITISH MUSEUM  PRESS

Published by British Museum Press
A division of The British Museum
Company Ltd
46 Bloomsbury Street, London
WC1B 3QQ

First published 1991
Second edition 2000

Julian Reade has asserted his right
to be identified as the author of this
work.

A catalogue record for this book is
available from the British Library

ISBN 0 7141 2181 9

Designed by Martin Richards
Series design by Carroll Associates
Typeset in Van Dijck
Printed in Hong Kong by Imago

Right *Marsh scene in south-east
Mesopotamia, with date palms, reed
huts and a boat.*

Front cover *Sumerian feast and
supplies of food. From the Standard
of Ur (see p.52).*

Contents

1 Introduction *6*

2 Towards agriculture *14*

3 Towards cultural segregation *18*

4 Towards civilization *28*

5 The emergence of city states *38*

6 From estate to empire *62*

7 The emegence of the individual *74*

8 Epilogue *84*

Further reading *88*

Chronology *89*

List of illustrations with dimensions *93*

Index *95*

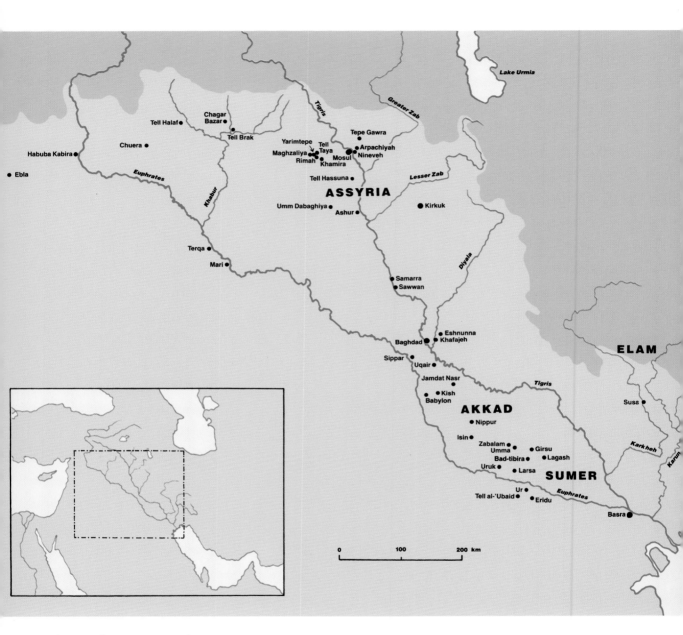

1 *Map of Mesopotamia, showing
selected ancient sites. The area
shown in brown is approximately
1000 m above sea level or higher.*

Preface

With the close of the most recent Ice Age, the region between Egypt, India and southern Central Asia provided an environment which was exploited with unprecedented success by mankind and the other species with which mankind established a working relationship. Many of the principal developments, crucial in world history, were centred on Mesopotamia. This book offers my view of the more significant factors in the process. It is concerned only with early Mesopotamia, before 1500 BC. The written and material evidence surviving from this region is far more abundant than can be indicated here. Books in the Further Reading list on page 88 should be consulted for alternative approaches.

Chapter One | Introduction

Traditionally, in the Western world, real civilization is thought to begin with the Romans and the Greeks. They are seen as the people who brought the art of writing to Europe, who introduced cities and roads, science and written laws: effectively the whole apparatus of organization and bureaucracy which are envisaged as the essential elements of material civilization. The names of European cities are not recorded before the Greco-Roman period, and Herodotus, the earliest Greek historian whose writings survive (dating from the fifth century BC), is accordingly known as the Father of History.

This simple view of the past ignores both the prehistory of Europe itself and those oriental cultures which stood behind Rome and Greece, flourishing thousands of years before the Parthenon was built in Athens or the Pantheon in Rome. It is to these earlier cultures, extending from Egypt to India, that we must look for the real beginnings of Western civilization, for the original establishment of a dominant network of villages and cities across the natural wilderness. Egypt is the best known of these cultures, because its monuments were built in an environment tailor-made for eternity, while the first civilization of India with its undeciphered script will long remain the most mysterious. Among them all, however, Mesopotamia occupies central place.

This name, Mesopotamia, meant originally the land between the rivers Tigris and Euphrates. It has acquired now a more practical meaning, referring broadly to the territories adjoining the Tigris and Euphrates and their principal confluents, mainly the downstream plains and valleys rather than the mountains where the rivers rise. This covers most of modern Iraq and north-east Syria, and part of south-east Turkey.

The flood-plain of south Iraq, watered by the two rivers and virtually flat, was the home of Sumerian and Babylonian civilization. This civilization extended north-west, up the narrow plain of the Euphrates, deep into Syria. It also followed the Tigris into north Iraq, known as Assyria, a region of rolling hills and plains which reach westward back into Syria towards the Euphrates. This is all part of the land sometimes called the Fertile Crescent, a favoured area where for thousands of years agricultural communities have repeatedly developed and prospered. On the north and east, in Turkey and towards Iran, this region encounters high mountain ranges. In the south, and in many places between the two rivers, there is dry steppe or desert.

Situated as it was, ancient Mesopotamia was never an isolated region. It had few natural resources of its own besides what could be got from agriculture, but it had ready access to the minerals of Turkey, Iran and the Gulf. There were no significant natural obstacles to travel across the plains, and there were passes through the hill country. So Mesopotamia was open to influences from without, and developments within Mesopotamia were in turn liable to affect neighbouring regions. During prehistory the peoples of Mesopotamia were among the first

successful farmers, producing the regular supplies of food on which civilization has come to depend, and during 3000-500 BC Mesopotamia was
one of the leading centres of literacy in the world. Otherwise expressed,
that is about half the length of time in the history of mankind for which
contemporary written records exist at all. Whatever has happened since
in human history tends to have precedents in ancient Mesopotamia.

Much of our evidence for that huge length of time comes from con-
ventional archaeology, from observations and excavations of buildings,
settlements and landscapes, and from objects made from solid materials
such as stone, metal and clay. Archaeologists interested in the prehistoric
periods have examined a great variety of sites, while those concerned
with periods after 3500 BC have tended to concentrate on the most
prominent structures such as palaces and temples. In either case we
possess only a modest proportion of the information that is potentially
available in the soil, and we have to allow for possible distortions
resulting either from the inadequacy of our evidence or from defective
interpretation of what there is.

The soils and climate of Mesopotamia are not particularly
favourable to the preservation of organic remains such as textiles and
wood. Stone was used sparingly there. Architecture itself usually

2 *Zibliyat, an abandoned city on
an ancient branch of the Euphrates.*

3 *Administrative tablet in Sumerian recording cultic payments of grain for the goddess Bau. Dated to the fourth year of Uru-inim-gina, ruler of Lagash (about 2200 BC). From Girsu.*

employed a relatively perishable material, sun-dried brick. In one respect, however, Mesopotamia is uniquely favoured, and that is in the preservation of written records from the historical periods. These are the texts in the so-called cuneiform (wedge-shaped) script, inscribed on clay or stone. First made before 3000 BC, they become from 2500 BC onwards an outstandingly informative source for many aspects of Mesopotamian life.

These documents have often been found grouped together in archives. They include letters, stories, business contracts and memoranda, and scientific and religious records. Potentially they offer a detailed knowledge of the circumstances in which they were written, sometimes far more detailed than the knowledge available for relatively recent periods in, say, medieval Europe. There is always the danger of bias, because the accidents of discovery illuminate some areas while leaving others in possibly undeserved silence and obscurity, but that does not detract from the vital immediacy of the archives available for our inspection.

Some of these documents also provide our chronological framework for ancient Mesopotamia. History, as the term is widely understood today, incorporating the practical analysis of consecutive events and long-term processes, had precursors but no established place in the literary tradition of ancient Mesopotamia. Systematic records were usually kept, however, for various purposes including the maintenance of calendars, and these are an essential historical source. Individual years were named after memorable events, or after annual officials, or after the number of years that had elapsed since a king's accession. By combining lists of year names, of kings and of dynasties, the ancients calculated distances of time extending over many generations, and we can do the same. Naturally there are problems, such as gaps and confusing overlaps in the evidence, some of which have still to be resolved, but we now possess a chronological scheme going back to 1400 BC which is accurate within a few years, and not more than a century or two out with the earliest political records around 2400 BC.

For the thousands of years of prehistory no such confidence is possible. The technique of radiocarbon dating, which relies on the decay

4 Irrigated fields in the Euphrates valley, western Mesopotamia.

of radioactive isotopes in organic remains, gives a useful sense of the time-scales involved without, so far, any great claims to precision. The same applies to other scientific dating methods. Real accuracy may come in the end through dendrochronology, the study of tree-rings with their annual variability, which can help determine exactly when a tree was felled; but this technique depends on the recovery of timber from ancient buildings, and there is much research still to be done.

The landscape

South Mesopotamia or Babylonia, effectively southern Iraq, is a country where the past is a large component of the landscape. It appears as mounds, sometimes many metres high but more often extensive low humps and irregularities, which mark the sites of ancient towns and villages. It appears as ramparts of accumulated earth, curving into the distance, where irrigation canals have been dug and cleaned out year after year, continuously, until the heap has grown so high that a fresh canal has had to be dug alongside the old one. It appears, above all, in the vast areas where mismanagement of the irrigation system has left the fertile soil barren, saturated and encrusted with salt.

Yet this has always been a country of great potential wealth. Although rainfall is sparse and unreliable, the Tigris and Euphrates bring enough water to irrigate, through canals, a large proportion of the land, supplying some of the most extensive date plantations in the world, and giving abundant harvests of grain. There is fine pasture for animals, and fish in the rivers and marshes.

In north Mesopotamia the past has left a different legacy. There are the same massive mounds covering ancient settlements, but farmers have mainly relied on rainfall, without the perils and complications of irrigation. The harvest can be phenomenal and the pasture is superb. Here, as through much of the Middle East, the most significant effect of human activity on the landscape has been the destruction of trees and scrub

5 *Sumerian fisherman. From the Standard of Ur (see page 52). About 2400 BC.*

6 *Bitumen boat model which was placed loaded with goods in a grave at Ur, to supply the dead person or possibly to lure away an evil demon. Boats of a similar design can still be seen in the marshes of south Mesopotamia. About 2150 BC.*

7 *Part of a house model showing a sheep with a shaggy fleece on the corner of a roof. From north Mesopotamia. About 2200 BC.*

8 *Sumerians leading a bull. From the Standard of Ur. About 2400* BC.

9 *Terracotta head of a ewe, probably from the decoration of a temple at Uruk. About 3300-3000* BC.

for food, fuel, building or other purposes, with herds of goats preventing regeneration. Forest cover has been stripped from the foothills and the mountains, leading to erosion and the disappearance of perennial streams.

There was a time not so long ago, around 10,000 BC, when the natural resources of these regions, in both north and south Mesopotamia, must have seemed far more abundant and infinitely varied. We cannot draw, from the scrappy archaeological evidence of seeds, pollen and bone, any precise picture of the environment then, nor of how it was to change through the centuries that followed, but we may envisage an Assyrian landscape that ranged from thickly forested hills through open parkland to grassy steppe, and a Babylonian landscape in which the Tigris and Euphrates meandered endlessly through jungle, lagoon and marsh. In the plains there were herds of wild cattle, asses, gazelle and larger antelopes, and elephant; there were wild boar in the valleys, sheep and goats in the hills. While fluctuations in the pattern of rainfall in the north, and potentially drastic shifts in the courses of rivers in Babylonia, undoubtedly affected particular areas from time to time, man was only beginning to make his mark.

10 *Sumerian goat and sheep. From the Standard of Ur. About 2400 BC.*

Chapter Two | Towards agriculture

The prehistory of Mesopotamia is an exciting period which saw some of the most fundamental developments in the history of mankind. Yet many divergent interpretations of the evidence are possible, and much basic knowledge has still to be recovered. Two simple factors bear a considerable part of the responsibility.

One is that people have repeatedly, over thousands of years, chosen to settle in places which are naturally inviting, with good water, land and communications. The places with the best resources tend to become the most important centres, and even when such a place is abandoned for some good reason, it is usually reoccupied eventually. So, through interminable demolition and reconstruction, the remains of the early prehistoric settlements in the best positions have gradually been buried many metres below the surface. Even if they were all located and archaeologists anxious to excavate them were free to destroy the remains of later civilizations above, the demands on time and labour would be prohibitive.

The second factor which restricts research on the prehistoric period is that, in south Mesopotamia especially but also in parts of the north, many settlements have been buried by natural causes. The rivers carry quantities of silt which are deposited in the flood-plains, accumulating to such an extent over the centuries that the entire landscape is transformed. Though the effect is irregular, most of the small prehistoric sites of south Mesopotamia have been concealed in this way. Only a few have been discovered, a tiny percentage of those which undoubtedly exist.

Our information therefore derives mainly from small village settlements, which are easy to find in the north Mesopotamian steppe, and from a handful of sites elsewhere. Though hardly representative, these partial remains illustrate the fundamental subsistence activities of prehistoric people. Their beliefs and methods of social organization are less accessible.

The first few thousand years (say, 10,000-6000 BC, but dates at this remote period can easily be out by a thousand years or more) cover what is often called the Neolithic revolution. This term oversimplifies a complicated process that began earlier and is still incomplete today, but essentially it describes the critical phase during which man ceased to rely on hunting wild animals and collecting wild plants to eat, and instead came to rely mainly on herded animals and deliberately planted food crops.

The transition from hunting to herding is an obvious one, as people followed or waylaid animals on their seasonal migrations, and methodical exploitation became deliberate management. Often these activities involved movement over long distances, as animals needed food and water throughout the year. In Mesopotamia this might mean following the lush grass into the desert after the winter and spring rains,

and retiring to the river valleys and hills in summer and autumn. It is a way of life which makes excellent use of available resources, and it has persisted to this day.

Not all members of a hunting community, however, might need to move far. Campsites could be established in convenient places, especially places with access to a varied range of food resources. Skilfully chosen campsites would be used over many years. In particularly favoured locations, and in places close to rivers where fish were abundant, there might be little incentive for movement at all.

Around all these camps, at appropriate times of year, people would collect the best wild plants they could find to eat, and seeds of the preferred varieties were dropped, year in year out, at first inadvertently, in the same vicinity. The process of selection favoured the survival, around camps, of crop varieties preferred by man, and the deliberate encouragement and support of these varieties became, imperceptibly so far as we can observe the change, the practice of agriculture. What is more, unusually productive varieties of particular plants, which would not have flourished in the wild, might and did find human protection. Subsequently seeds could be, and were, transported to areas where they would not normally have grown at all. When adequate techniques of food storage had been developed, presumably through centuries or millennia of trial and error, there was practically no limit to the number of people who could reside permanently in one place as settled villagers instead of itinerant hunters and herdsmen.

It cannot be claimed that the process summarized above is a full explanation of the Neolithic revolution, which seems to have occurred independently in many parts of the world, but it is broadly compatible with the evidence that exists in and around Mesopotamia. It also points to the very early origin of one of the most characteristic features of Mesopotamian civilization, the antipathy and interrelationship of two kinds of lifestyle, one primarily dependent on herding and the other primarily dependent on cultivation. Usually, in the archaeological record, only the permanent settlements can be seen, solid monuments to the enviable success of those communities which practised agriculture at the same time as they kept animals. On the fringes of settled life, meanwhile, there were mobile communities, sometimes impoverished, sometimes virtual cities on the move, which maintained traditions of herding

11 *Stone frieze, framed in copper, from the Ninhursag temple facade at Tell al-'Ubaid. On the right a cow is being milked, while its muzzled calf looks on. In the centre is a farm shed. The men on the left, holding large jars and transferring liquid from one container to another, are probably making butter for storage. About 2300 BC.*

that went back before the Neolithic period. The settled cultivators increasingly looked down on the pastoralists as uncouth barbarians, but the barbarians periodically demonstrated that their way of life was more flexible and that they might be better able to survive in difficult circumstances.

An example of one of the earliest Mesopotamian settlements known, perhaps before 7000 BC, is Maghzaliya in north Iraq. Of the animal bones recovered from excavation there, some sixty per cent belonged to wild animals, and forty per cent to domesticated sheep and goats, with a few cattle. Plant remains included seeds of wheat, barley and lentil. This village evidently belonged to a late stage in the transition to farm-based subsistence, and the existence of a stone wall surrounding it suggests that human communities were already accustomed to protecting themselves from human rather than merely natural predators.

There were large quantities of obsidian at Maghzaliya. This material is a black volcanic glass, superior to flint for the manufacture of sharp tools, and it is found at various places in Turkey. However such goods were carried and distributed, through intermediaries or long-distance travellers, its presence at Maghzaliya is evidence for an export trade, and for a long-distance network of communications, which lasted through much of the prehistoric period. Similarly some copper, besides documenting the beginnings of metallurgy, may have a Turkish or Iranian origin.

Maghzaliya has also produced stone vessels, figurines and rectangular buildings of clay on stone foundations. All of these are the tangible relics of flourishing craft industries. Probably some day an archaeologist

12 *The beads in this necklace are arranged here as they were found on excavation. Six are made from obsidian, a volcanic glass which had to be brought from eastern Turkey. A seventh bead of dark clay imitates the shape of the obsidian ones. The cowrie shells will have come from the Gulf, and originally contained red ochre. There is also one stone pendant. From Arpachiyah. About 5000 BC.*

or bulldozer will locate one of the centres to which villages like Maghzaliya looked for leadership. There will be evidence for the production of luxury goods, cult statues and decorated architecture, comparable with sites such as Jericho in Palestine or Catal Huyuk in Turkey. This is a pattern which is constantly repeated in prehistoric Mesopotamia, with characteristics of a few small sites pointing to the existence of towns and elaborate socio-economic organizations. Anyone familiar with north Mesopotamia can suggest promising mounds likely to conceal some of the very earliest towns, and the stone statuettes found in early graves at Tell as-Sawwan in central Iraq hint at what should eventually emerge.

Another example dates from a later period, somewhere before 6000 BC. This is the village of Umm Dabaghiya, also in north Iraq, located on the very fringe of habitable land, where agriculture is impossible today and can only have been possible occasionally in the past at times of exceptional rainfall. By this date the farming of cereals is well attested in contemporary villages in areas with more water, and these were eaten and may have been grown at Dabaghiya. It seems, however, that the major activity of the inhabitants of this village was the hunting of wild asses and gazelle, and dried meat and leather could have been preserved in the extensive storerooms found there. Since both the people of Dabaghiya and contemporary farmers elsewhere used similar items of material culture, such as pottery containers decorated in specific styles, it is likely that there was a degree of economic integration over a broad area, with Dabaghiya specializing in the export of animal products.

Maghzaliya and Dabaghiya are just two of many early prehistoric settlements scattered from north Mesopotamia westward to the Mediterranean and the Turkish plateau, eastward through Iran, which had their local characteristics but which were clearly in communication with their neighbours or formed parts of significantly larger social organizations. What forms these organizations took we cannot know, but comparison with people grouped in remote villages today suggests that at one time or another there will have been a huge range of possibilities, from small-scale despotism to primitive democracy, dependent on local circumstances and personalities. Tribal relationships, based on real or supposed common ancestry, were probably of great significance.

Chapter Three | Towards cultural segregation

In later prehistory, from around 6000 BC on, it becomes increasingly easy to classify settlements over extensive areas of Mesopotamia as belonging to specific cultures. Such classification has conventionally been based on just one facet of material culture, the pottery. Baked clay containers had been made before 6000 BC, but from then on the technology of controlled firing that is necessary to create them was becoming more generally available. Once this was so, ceramic pots were evidently easier to make than stone containers, and they were more durable than those of skin or wood. Once broken and beyond repair, they remained as virtually imperishable fragments scattered around ancient sites. Since the ways in which pots were made, decorated and used changed over the centuries, sites can be assigned approximate dates on the basis merely of the sherds lying on their surfaces. The cultures are accordingly named after the sites, such as Tell Hassuna, Tell Halaf, and Tell al-'Ubaid, where the corresponding kinds of pottery were first excavated and recognized as significant.

For instance, Hassuna pottery is most readily recognized by a few simple shapes which presumably reflect the ways in which the containers were used; it is well fired, with decoration of slashed incisions or neatly painted lines. It was identified at Tell Hassuna in north Iraq, a site lying in what is now fertile farmland, with crops and livestock dependent on rainfall. The remains indicated that this had been, in the Hassuna period, an agricultural village where the material conditions of life were in some ways not vastly different from those of modern villages in the same region. Hassuna potsherds had been found before, in the earliest levels of

13 Painted pottery: bowl and jar in the Samarra style. From Samarra. About 5500 BC.

18

a deep sounding at the great site of Nineveh, but it was at Hassuna itself that their cultural context was more fully examined and understood. Since sherds in the Hassuna style or comparable styles are found at many north Mesopotamian sites that were probably similar agricultural villages, these define the extent of the Hassuna culture and period. Although a rough-and-ready definition, it has proved workable in practice.

Samarra pottery, in contrast, which also has its distinctive shapes and more elaborate painted decoration, is named after the site of Samarra in central Iraq (better known as an Islamic capital city and shrine). Samarra potsherds have been found at Hassuna, Nineveh and elsewhere in north Iraq, where they overlie and may overlap the end of the Hassuna period. There is no straight progression, however, from one style to the other, as Samarra sites seem to be far commoner and better established in central Iraq. One possibility, then, is that this pottery was produced by people whose main original centres were indeed in the Samarra region, where farming cannot rely on rainfall alone, and that their agriculture included the irrigation of crops in the alluvial Tigris-Euphrates flood-plain, which begins at this point to broaden as the rivers approach Babylonia.

The Hassuna and Samarra pottery styles might then represent two methods of subsistence which were substantially different from one another in some ways but sufficiently similar, in the need for land and other natural resources, for serious competition to develop between the peoples practising them. So the extension of the Samarra pottery style into north Iraq would indicate the success of one group of people at the expense of the other, and could be taken as the first visible instance of conflict between the peoples of north Mesopotamia and those living further south, a theme which recurs over and over again at later dates.

Yet it is debatable whether such strong conclusions can be based on a few crates of broken pottery. Opponents of this scheme can point to the likelihood that pots were handmade by women, who might continue working in familiar ways after moving to new homes, and that such movements can result from marriage alliances and capture as well as from wholesale conquest. Moreover, traditional practices can survive in physically or socially isolated communities long after they have been abandoned elsewhere. Any interpretation of the evidence from prehistoric Mesopotamia can usually be supported by some parallel drawn from the voluminous anthropological literature on tribal Africa or the Pacific. If it is plain that Samarra superseded Hassuna, thereby demonstrating greater power of survival, it is wholly uncertain what this meant in human terms.

The assumption that a shared pottery style is not merely convenient but crucial for classifying groups of prehistoric Mesopotamian sites has found strong support as research has continued on the Halaf culture, about 5500-5000 BC, which followed Hassuna in north Mesopotamia, again overlapping Samarra.

Halaf is named after Tell Halaf in north Syria. Again the pottery has its distinctive shapes, reflecting usage. The smaller vessels represent what has been perhaps the finest tradition of hand-made pottery in the

14 Above *The Halaf period potters produced some of the finest wares known from the ancient world. Vessels in the distinctive style of these plates, shaped by hand, well fired, and painted with imaginative designs, were made throughout north Mesopotamia. From Arpachiyah. About 5000 BC.*

world; they are thin-walled but strong, with complicated and imaginative designs painted in one or more colours. Because of its quality, sherds of this ware are easily recognized, and their recorded distribution, from the Mediterranean coast to Iran, is greater than might have been the case otherwise. Sites of this period that have been excavated in north Mesopotamia, however, turn out to have much more in common than styles of pottery container: there are similarities in food, technology, architecture, ritual practices and ornament, which come together to suggest something much more far-reaching. For instance, the village buildings can be rectangular, as is usual in other periods, but there are some round huts with entrance passages – an odd and highly distinctive keyhole ground-plan. With the aid of this extra criterion, we can draw the boundaries of the Halaf culture to cover all north Mesopotamia including the upper Tigris valley in Turkey, which helps account for a Halaf presence as far north as Lake Van and Soviet Armenia. This is the territory where dialects of the Hurrian language were subsequently at home. While we really know little about how the inhabitants of a Halaf village thought, let alone what language or languages they used for thinking, and what levels of abstraction could be expressed verbally, it seems likely that the natives of Tell Halaf itself in Syria, and of Arpachiyah in Iraq, will have had comparable social structures, sharing

15 Left *Schematic stone figure, with virtually no arms or legs, and a small head, but exaggerated sexual organs. From Arpachiyah. About 5000 BC.*

16 Right *Figurines of terracotta or unbaked clay were made during the Halaf period, probably for magical or religious purposes. The women often have large breasts and hips, emphasizing motherhood. This example is decorated with black paint apparently representing bangles on the arms and legs, a loincloth, and painted or tattooed breasts. From Chagar Bazar. About 5000 BC.*

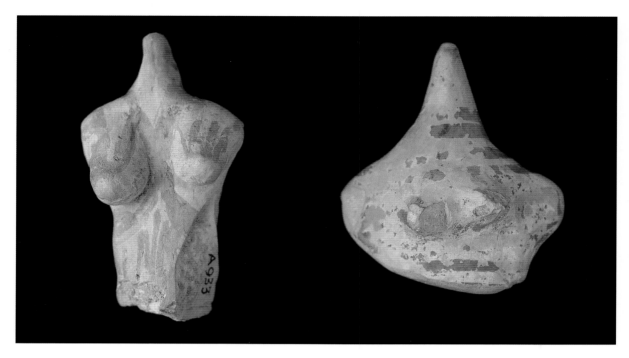

17 *Female figurines of painted terracotta, the right-hand one pierced for use as a pendant or amulet. Such figurines, with their schematic heads, probably represent a goddess of motherhood and fertility, the supreme giver of life worshipped in agricultural and other communities throughout the Near East and elsewhere. She corresponds to a goddess later known by various names, notably Ishtar. From Arpachiyah. About 5000 BC.*

18 *Terracotta heads of two women. From Tell al-'Ubaid and an unidentified site. About 4500 BC.*

many of the same implicit values, and that even those who did not travel regularly may have met from time to time in religious or administrative centres.

At the same time, the Halaf culture need not be regarded as entirely cohesive and all-embracing within the area it covered. Groups of the population such as mobile herdsmen, who are less easy than villagers for archaeologists to trace, remain undefined. The sheer difficulty of setting fires and cutting trees with stone axes will have restricted human access to much of the countryside. The horns of cattle loom large in Halaf

19 *Many pottery vessels of the Halaf period are decorated with elaborate patterns including animals which range in style from naturalistic to highly schematic. Some were probably made for magical use, but it is seldom possible to assess the symbolic value of prehistoric art with any degree of confidence. The spotted animals may be leopards. The bull's head and horns, highly schematized, are a common theme, reflecting the size and power of the wild oxen which were still widespread at the time; horns became symbols of divinity in historic Mesopotamia. Snakes were also potent symbols. From Arpachiyah. About 5000 BC.*

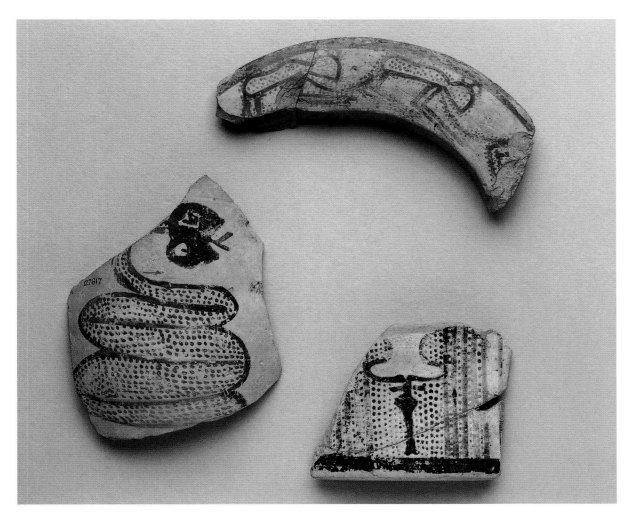

20 *Dish in the Ubaid pottery style. From Ur.*
About 4000 BC.

pottery design; some were domesticated, but wild oxen and carnivores must have been abundant, masters of their own territory, the embodiment of power beyond human control.

Meanwhile, in south Mesopotamia, a radically different way of life was established, reflected incidentally but most usefully in another entirely different tradition of pottery-making. The site of Tell al-'Ubaid, after which this ceramic style is named, lies in the far south-east of Mesopotamia, close to the point where the Euphrates plain merges into marshland as it approaches the sea. It is possibly in this region that the date palm was domesticated, with systematic harnessing of a natural process whereby the river water is regularly pushed back upstream by the tides and can be diverted into a network of canals, with palm groves alongside them. Fishing, and the exploitation of the sea, were also important in prehistoric south Mesopotamia, and one of the earliest known buildings of the Ubaid period to have been excavated had a pile of fish upon its floor. In due course, however, probably the most important element in the south Mesopotamian economy came to be the cultivation of food crops, notably wheat and barley, which had originally been domesticated closer to the habitats of their natural progenitors in north Mesopotamia. The difference was that in the south they relied on irrigation, a difficult process since the annual floods seldom arrive at the best time for farmers, but one which does make possible, with proper management and the best strains, outstanding yields. Similarly, flocks of sheep and goats flourished in south Mesopotamia, though their wild ancestors had come from hillier northern regions.

The evidence hints at a considerable degree of state organization developing in south Mesopotamia during the Ubaid period, from 5500 BC on, but it is difficult to assess since most remains are deeply buried and are not necessarily identified during archaeological survey. A substantial Ubaid settlement, for instance, at Uqair, was only found because a later building was being excavated above, and it remains one of a handful of Ubaid sites recorded in the upper half of the Tigris Euphrates flood-plain. In the far south, on the other hand, the evidence is more abundant, and the excavators at Eridu made what seems a crucial discovery.

The city of Eridu lies close to what may once have been the seashore, and in historical times it was regarded as a city of great antiquity and religious significance, home of Enki, who was effectively the Sumerian god of the sea as well as the god of wisdom. It was inhabited as late as 2500 BC, but after this period tended to be restored and maintained chiefly as a historical shrine. Its time of greatness was then prehistoric, and excavations below its temple-tower uncovered a sequence of occupation which went back three thousand years and which was marked by a notable degree of continuity in the material culture. It has even been suggested that the cult of Enki, marked in historical times by the massive temple, could be traced back to a meagre hut of the early Ubaid period. So, on one level, the societies of south Mesopotamia up to the late Ubaid period, around 4000 BC, and for a further thousand years or more, practised a long-established way of life, less liable to disintegration or drastic interruption than was the case with the contemporary societies of north Mesopotamia.

The reasons why one type of social organization survives better than another are seldom straightforward. Obviously competitive adaptation is the key, but archaeological finds do not necessarily explain why one particular system has the edge. We can be well informed about subsistence methods, specialized skills, domestic arrangements and even about the social status of individuals in different graves, without beginning to penetrate the underpinning ideology. In the case of the Ubaid culture, however, we can see that it was indeed materially successful. The

21 *Flocks coming home. From Uruk. About 3300-3000 BC.*

22 *Terracotta figurines of women from south Mesopotamia are strikingly slim in contrast to those from the north. This one shows a woman suckling a child. Both have bands of paint around neck and waist, presumably beads or similar decoration, and the woman has bracelets. As is usual with these figurines, paint is also applied to the woman's shoulders and to her nipples. The child's head has the elongated shape and prominent eyes characteristic of Ubaid figurines. From Ur. About 4500 BC.*

reasons are likely to include, as in Egypt, the sheer size and homogeneity of the south Mesopotamian plain in which it developed, the number of settlements, which were sufficiently abundant to shrug off local setbacks, and the basic reliability of the water supply, which was capricious in its effects but never liable to failure. So, once prehistoric agricultural communities were established in south Mesopotamia, they could expand more steadily and fully, over the centuries, than was the case in the north. Moreover, even if outsiders did move into south Mesopotamia, as may have happened from time to time in prehistory as it certainly did subsequently, they were disarmed and absorbed by the nature of the landscape which imposed, for long-term survival, the necessity for hard-won techniques of irrigation which only the resilient natives knew.

The situation in north Mesopotamia was simpler and more volatile, and the history of later times offers a likely parallel for prehistoric developments. Essentially the farming communities which rely on the cultivation of arable crops have always survived in some areas, but they are liable to find themselves exploited by semi-nomadic groups of herdsmen coming either from the hills or from the desert fringes. There are many competitors for the same range of resources. In times of stress; such as prolonged drought, the poverty of the farmer is compounded by the desperation of the shepherd. The landscape is more fragmented than in south Mesopotamia, and social organizations, though they may flourish and establish themselves for substantial intervals of time, remain more brittle and vulnerable than in the coherent south. There is a comparable contrast between Mesopotamia as a whole and the still more fragile cultures of ancient Iran and Turkey.

We accordingly find, in north Mesopotamia, repeated evidence for the virtual abandonment, by arable farmers, of some of the most fertile but insecure areas, and the changes from one period to another are relatively clear-cut, with a notable shortage of transitional phases in the material culture. Undoubtedly there were such transitions, but the evidence for them is elusive because it will be located mainly in refuge areas which have enjoyed greater security and concomitant density of settlement at many periods. Thus excavations at Tepe Gawra in north Iraq, in a locality whose natural security is demonstrated by the exceptionally long-established nature of the local population even today, have produced a much fuller archaeological sequence than has been possible in the more vulnerable areas, those most exposed to damage from decreased levels of rainfall. An example of the latter is Yarimtepe, again in north Iraq but on the fringe of the desert steppe. Yarimtepe occupies a typical position for a prehistoric village, at the confluence of two watercourses. There are three distinct mounds, of which one has Hassuna remains from top to bottom, one has Halaf remains virtually from top to bottom, and the third is predominantly Ubaid. While there is modest evidence for the transitions between these periods, it is almost as if the site had been abandoned in the intervals, and then repossessed by people who chose to build on fresh flat ground instead of on an inconveniently high old mound. Pastoralists who must have been there in the intervals have left few traces of their passing.

Chapter Four | Towards civilization

The contrast between south and north Mesopotamia, between relatively stable and unstable environments, had far-reaching consequences. It became a recurrent feature that the south influenced the north rather than vice versa. The prehistory and history of the south offer a comprehensible sequence of innovations and developments that can be appreciated without heavy reference to the world outside. Some innovations came from the north, but it often seems barbarous and backward by comparison, a view which the inhabitants of the south were inclined to share.

The first unmistakable evidence of this is the spread of Ubaid pottery to the north, ousting Halaf, perhaps about 5000 BC. There is a partial technical explanation for the development, in that Ubaid pots were being made on a slow wheel which facilitated manufacture and repetitive decoration, so that the process of production seems to have been more economical than it had been for hand-made Halaf ceramics. There were far more substantial changes, however. One of the most startling is the eventual construction, at Gawra, of a building with distinctive features of plan and decoration that correspond to those of a south Mesopotamian temple. The unity of the Halaf area disintegrates. The simplest available explanation is that a significant disturbance in the equilibrium of Halaf society, the result of internal evolution or external pressure, had opened the way to an invasion of ideas from the south, and quite possibly an invasion of people too. A possible cause is direct rivalry stemming from the economic success of the south. However that may be, we have a re-enactment of the spread of Samarra pottery, prefiguring a succession of south-north confrontations which are, like the encounter between nomad and peasant, commonplace themes of Mesopotamian history.

Effectively what seems to have happened, time and again, is that the massive resources of the south, through efficient management of the rivers, led to population growth, tighter organization of society, and consequently the concentration of power in the hands of the administrators, the rulers. We have no reason to suppose that one model of state organization prevailed in prehistory, but similar constraints will have operated whether or not the administrators had the consent of their subordinates. The significant factor here is the economic and hence the military strength of the south when compared with the north, where power was more diffuse.

One incentive for southern interest in other areas was the lack of natural resources in the south. Good timber was wanted from the hill country, all the more so as copper had become increasingly available, from about 4000 BC on, for cutting down trees. Copper itself, for tools and weapons, had to be obtained from Turkey, Iran or the Gulf. So did gold, other metals and precious stones. Such items might have been obtained originally through prehistoric patterns of trade or exchange.

Eventually they were to be obtained through intimidation, a progression from peaceful commerce to war that has been common enough in world history, but exactly when the process began is arguable.

At one stage it was proposed that there was clear evidence for it, towards the end of the Uruk period, with the appearance at Habuba Kabira, on the middle Euphrates, of a colony from south Iraq. That was one explanation for the existence there of a walled town whose material culture was more or less identical with that of south Mesopotamia. It seemed to be a cultural intrusion, unrelated to the native culture of the region at the time. Possible explanations for its presence would include overpopulation in south Mesopotamia, with deliberate emigration, and the establishment of strongholds on the way from south Mesopotamia to the north-western regions, where raw materials such as timber and copper were to be found An alternative explanation is that the middle Euphrates valley and south Mesopotamia showed a single culture.

The existence of trading colonies or more modest settlements can be inferred from the discovery, both in north Mesopotamia and on the Iranian plateau, of evidence for the use of distinctive recording systems. This evidence is in the shape of unbaked tablets of clay which, while still damp, have been marked with primitive numerals and sealed, as a guarantee, by cylindrical seals rolled across their surface. These tablets

23 Cylinder seals were introduced around 3500 BC. They served the same purposes as stamp seals, to identify people or institutions, but their designs were rolled on to clay instead of being impressed into it and could be applied more satisfactorily to large areas such as sealed doors. This example is made of steatite, with a glazed surface that resulted from heating the stone. Many lumps of clay sealed with comparable geometric designs have been found at Nineveh. About 2900 BC.

24 *Bevelled-rim bowls, hand-made in moulds and exceptionally crude, have been found in such large numbers throughout Mesopotamia that they provide impressive evidence for relationships between sites many hundreds of miles apart. They may have been used for rations of food allocated to workers. The shape is perhaps derived from that of bowls made from compressed leaves, such as can still be seen in central India. From Nineveh. About 3300-3000 BC.*

are administrative records, shortly preceding the introduction of writing proper, and they are also present in south Mesopotamia, at Uruk. We do not really know where the system was invented, but the close resemblance in the styles of the seals confirms that we are looking at a phenomenon that overrode local cultural differences.

Perhaps the most striking example of the wide spread of some features of the Uruk culture consists in the distribution of what must be one of the crudest ceramic forms ever made, the so-called bevelled-rim bowl. This kind of bowl, mould-made and mass-produced, is found in large numbers throughout Mesopotamia and beyond. Its place of invention is unknown, but it came to be locally manufactured everywhere. Various explanations have been offered for its popularity, including the suggestions that it was used in the salt trade and that it had some magical or religious function, reflecting a widely adopted cult. The main possibility, however, seems to be that it was employed for the allocation of food rations, and was frequently discarded immediately after use, like the aluminium foil containing a modern take-away meal. If this is correct, it implies that comparable systems for the distribution of food, involving to some extent the centralized organization of labour and supplies, existed wherever bevelled-rim bowls are found. Even if this explanation is incorrect, the distribution of the bowls remains solid evidence for long-distance similarities.

One model for a system which involved the centralized allocation of food rations is to be found at the site in south Mesopotamia after which the Uruk period is named. The name for once is apt, since Uruk was clearly a place of great importance at the time. There were probably other centres of comparable status, but Uruk happens to be the one that has been most fully excavated. It is the embodiment of developments that had been proceeding, if not uninterruptedly, at least without significant interruption, since the Ubaid period.

At Uruk, then, over most of the fourth millennium BC, there was a succession of elaborate buildings that can only have been created by large numbers of people working, freely or otherwise, together. Originally, it seems, when gods first acquired buildings of their own to inhabit, they occupied houses which were not substantially different from those of other inhabitants of a settlement. The maintenance of such buildings is likely to have become a communal obligation, and ultimately, in one way or another, temples acquired extensive property rights. In the course of centuries, temples were repeatedly reconstructed. The new constructions incorporated within themselves the ruins of the old, gradually accumulating platforms on which the latest version of each temple stood. Eventually the platform itself became a feature of temple architecture, especially in the most important religious centres, the prototype of the temple-tower or ziggurat which is the most characteristic feature of Mesopotamian religious architecture in historical times. This evolution is a telling illustration of the loyalty and respect for the past that repeatedly appear, with occasional dramatic exceptions, throughout Mesopotamian history. One such exception is found at Uruk itself, where an entire religious complex was demolished, for reasons about which we can only speculate.

Some of the buildings near the temple-towers at Uruk were evidently too big for ordinary domestic use, but their functions remain uncertain. A type of decoration found on several facades is the cone mosaic, consisting of patterns made by pressing coloured cones into wall-plaster to create patterns like those of woven reed-mat hangings. It is an odd and highly distinctive art-form which is attested throughout south Mesopotamia and sporadically in the north, emphasizing yet again the extent of southern cultural influence.

Other forms of artistic production attested at Uruk were also imitated elsewhere, but the high quality and variety of the Uruk finds suggests that their concentration at this site is not accidental. They include carvings on stone which range from large-scale boulders, with figures half life-size, to cylinder seals with miniature figures a couple of centimetres high. In this period people and animals are represented in a manner approaching realism, in contrast to the schematic or imaginative distortions of most prehistoric art. The large Uruk carvings were probably all created for religious reasons, as part of the decoration of a temple area. The same may apply to the elaborately carved or inlaid vessels that are also characteristic of this period. On a more practical level, this is a period when pottery for general use was being mass-produced with casual mastery on the fast wheel. Clearly these objects were no longer the result of home craftsmanship but were produced by professional specialists working under or close to organizations large enough to afford such luxuries. There is indeed evidence for the existence not only of specialized craftsmen, but also of specialized organizations dealing, for instance, with specific jobs

25 Hundreds of these miniature stone figurines, heavily emphasizing the eye, were found in the remains of the Eye Temple at Tell Brak, where they had probably been placed as votive deposits. They probably represent worshippers. About 3300 BC.

26 This is a typical pottery jar of the Jamdat Nasr (Late Uruk) type. Its place of discovery illustrates the contacts between Mesopotamia and the Oman peninsula, which was an important source of copper. From the Al-'Ain region, United Arab Emirates. About 3000 BC.

27 The symbol of the rosette was used in ancient Mesopotamia for protection and good luck. This is one of several stone rosettes that were probably mounted on the internal and external walls of the Eye Temple at Tell Brak. About 3000 BC.

28 *Gypsum head representing a god, goddess or worshipper. A vertical groove at the back of the head, with nail holes on the sides, suggests that it was originally fixed to a pole. From an early phase of the Eye Temple, Tell Brak. About 3300 BC.*

29 *Large numbers of stone and shell amulets, and stamp seals usually showing stylized animals, have been found at sites of the Late Uruk period. The seals have simple drilled designs on the base, also representing animals. Impressions of these seals have not been found, though they could have been used to stamp designs on perishable objects such as textiles. Shallow holes on the surface were inlaid with colour. From Tell Brak, Uruk, and unidentified sites. About 3300-3000 BC.*

such as textile production or farm administration. Moreover there is evidence for metalworking, and for the import of copper from the Gulf region, a trade reflected in the appearance of very late Uruk pottery as far away as Oman.

There is then at Uruk, before 3000 BC, the blurred outline of a comprehensible city state. The government was probably grounded in a religious ideology inherited from centuries past, and surplus resources went into the creation of temples rather than palaces or pyramids. There was a substantial degree of social stratification and probably regimentation and dissatisfaction. The population may have been small – one estimate was as low as 10,000 persons, though 50,000 carries more conviction – but Uruk exemplified a culture that spread throughout all Mesopotamia and part of southern Iran, and there were presumably more such cities. On this basis, through endless vicissitudes, Mesopotamian civilization was built.

The invention of writing

There is one innovation of the Uruk period, however, whose importance far exceeds any other, and which vastly enhanced the cultural continuity which south Mesopotamia, through its size and natural resilience, already enjoyed. This is the invention of a true writing system, a flexible method of recording language that had and retains limitless potential.

Several factors contributed to the emergence of writing. One was the need to define responsibility for goods, reflected in the use of personal or official seals from at least the Halaf period on. A second was the need to keep accounts, reflected from the Ubaid period in the use of tokens for recording quantities, and subsequently in the sealed numerical tablets. There was even a marriage of these techniques, in the shape of hollow clay tablets that contained numbers of tokens. It is also likely that some tokens had specific shapes to represent particular things such as sheep: the assumption is, for instance, that a shepherd was answerable for the number of sheep represented by tokens which were sealed, with a unique seal, in one hollow tablet. An alternative was to draw an animal on a clay tablet, with a numeral beside it. No doubt there were many experiments in record-keeping. The system that emerged as the most efficient, however, was a modified kind of picture-writing. Effectively each word was represented by a sign that might or might not be a recognizable pictogram with some visible relationship to its practical meaning.

The earliest known tablets written in this way have been found at Uruk. Their dating is arguable, with a maximum range of about 3500-3000 BC. It is just possible that they represent one moment of invention, but it seems more probable that the script had previously evolved through several phases from more straightforward pictograms. The subject matter of the clay tablets is largely administrative, with lists of officials and goods; there are also lists of signs, works of reference that could have been useful for both experienced and apprentice scribes. The language of the texts is probably Sumerian, though the pictographic nature of the script makes this hard to prove; one of the strongest arguments is the continuity of the reference texts from the Uruk period into historical times. The signs themselves were written in rows of boxes arranged from right to left.

Something that is absent from these tablets is personality. They are official documents. Similarly, the cylinder seals of the period represent specific themes but are not inscribed. There is a strong possibility that they were institutional seals, used by people in their official capacity rather than as individuals. Not until several centuries had passed, so far as we know, around 2400 BC, had writing been developed far enough to be used satisfactorily to express the grammatical complexities of spoken language and personal involvement.

Nonetheless we know that, in reality, individuals controlled the institutions. The priest who delivered offerings to his god received them from workers of a lower status. Competition between individuals also extended to competition between different groups of people, presumably

30 *Chart showing the evolution of writing, from pictogram to schematic cuneiform sign. At first the signs were written from the top downwards, in boxes arranged from right to left. A tablet written in this way can be turned so that its top edge is at the left: the signs then seem to have been written from left to right, in boxes arranged from the top downwards. Between 2400 and 1600 BC, the method of writing from left to right, in successive lines, gradually prevailed. The change of axis did not make the signs less legible, since by then they had lost their resemblance to pictures.*

BEFORE 3000 BC	ABOUT 3000 BC	ABOUT 2400 BC	ABOUT 1700 BC	
				SAG Head
				NINDA Food ration
				GU to eat
				AB Cow
				APIN Plough
				KI Place

31 *Administrative clay tablet. The deep circles and crescents impressed in the clay are numerals. The pictographic signs include several in the shape of jars with high necks; one sign, in the bottom row on the left, shows a bowl tipped towards a schematic human head. About 3000 BC.*

32 *Shell inlay of a priest offering a libation. Shell inlays, often combined with stone, were a standard Sumerian method of decorating the surface of wooden items such as fine musical instruments and pieces of furniture. From Ur. About 2400 BC.*

traditional struggles for the use of land or water. While one theme of Uruk art was the hunting of wild animals, which symbolized the protection of civilization from the wilderness, another was the killing of people in war. With the institutionalization of warfare, the people of prehistoric Mesopotamia had successfully completed the transition from savagery to civilization.

Chapter Five | The emergence of city states

Mesopotamian history until about 3000 BC can be treated as a continuous process of development, although, of course, in some ways this is an oversimplification. We simply do not know what calamities, intrusive ideologies or revolutionary trends may have unbalanced some of the illiterate societies of prehistory. Viewed from a distance, however, the development is relatively straightforward. In the south there was coherent growth of population, with steadily increasing exploitation of the natural resources. In the north there was a series of cultures which had much in common even if they were not themselves continuous, and which displayed increasingly close connections with the emergent civilization of the south.

After 3000 BC, however, as the archaeological evidence becomes more abundant, and written documents begin to provide something of a running commentary on events, Mesopotamian civilization can be seen to develop in cycles of alternating consolidation and disintegration. The scholar today, fingering broken pottery and naming a date for the abandonment of a mound or the breakdown of a canal, is apt to rationalize these changes with broad hypothetical generalizations, some of which are bound to be over-ambitious. The ancient Mesopotamians, who experienced these events in person, explained them in their own way with disconcerting immediacy. There are several such accounts. What may be the best of them was written about 2000 BC as the epic of Atrahasis, ostensibly a story about the origins of man but telling far more about how real men actually lived and died.

In the beginning, it seems, the gods had to do their own work, digging and clearing canals. This is a vivid reflection of what came to be the essential unending task, the daily grind of existence, of the farmer in south Mesopotamia. Not surprisingly, the gods eventually became tired of their work, threw down or destroyed their tools, and attacked the house of their manager: again an illustration of what was liable to happen in reality, when labourers felt themselves pressed too hard. On this occasion the solution was the creation of mankind, formed from an amalgam of clay and a god's flesh and blood.

Before too long, though, there was the problem of overpopulation. Mankind had multiplied so much that the gods were unable to sleep for the noise. The gods then made no fewer than four attempts to control their creation. The first involved sending a plague; the second involved the denial of rain, with drought as a consequence; the nature of the third is unclear, but its effects included the salination of the land, with resultant crop failure and famine severe enough to have parents eating their own children. These are not imaginary crises but the kinds of situations faced by real people that recurred at intervals throughout Mesopotamian history. It is perfectly plain that, just as the natural growth of population had gradually peopled the land during prehistory, so this trend continued with or without additional invaders or economic migrants.

The author of Atrahasis was describing problems which were all too familiar to his audience.

The gods made a final attempt to destroy mankind by sending a flood. This is one version of a story whose popularity in the ancient world is attested by biblical and other counterparts. On this occasion Atrahasis is the hero who, warned by his god, loads his household and his animals on to an ark and thereby survives the disaster. After this the gods appreciate that they do need mankind to perform the work for which it was created, and they decide to limit the population more systematically through childlessness, infant deaths, and the institution of ritual celibacy. One might have expected, at this point in the story, a

33 *Mountain range (Mount Nisir or Nimush), north-east of Kirkuk, on which the ark in the Babylonian story grounded after the flood.*

reference to the types of population control, such as the killing of unwanted children, which have been widely practised in societies lacking more sophisticated procedures. We may surmise, from the classic account of the abandoned child who grows up to be a hero, that this kind of thing did happen often enough in the ancient world, but it is not evident on a regular basis in historical Mesopotamia. Perhaps this was in any case an inappropriate subject for the Atrahasis epic, which deals not with human choice but with divine caprice.

The flood is the gods' most serious attempt to destroy their own creation, and it in turn is a reflection of reality. There had been a time when the melting of the winter snows in the mountains swelled the lower rivers and filled the lagoons of Mesopotamia as an annual blessing. The accelerated run-off resulting from deforestation in the uplands, however, coupled with the straightening and rationalization of water-courses downstream for the purposes of irrigation, effectively meant that additional water had to pass through tighter channels. There had always been floods, as the rivers expanded beyond their banks, but now there were artificial dams awaiting rupture. Anyone who has seen the Tigris or Euphrates in flood will appreciate the plight of the people

directly affected. First there is hope that the flood will not reach the homestead, followed by the frantic effort to drive protesting livestock and carry possessions beyond the reach of the water, and finally the long wait in improvised shelter until the waters subside and people can struggle through mud and slime back to their sagging homes and rebuild their lives. This, then, was the direct experience of the Sumerian farmer, and it must often have seemed doubtful whether the gods responsible would relent before the entire world was drowned.

Archaeologists have found traces of such floods, and the more imaginative minds have identified one or another episode as the agony of Atrahasis or Noah. On the whole, however, centres of population will have contained areas which remained above water level and gave a degree of security. A more serious long-term problem was the maintenance of the irrigation systems in the face of this kind of disruption, since every attempt to improve the situation brought with it the risk of making things worse.

This is what happened, on a massive scale, sometime about 3000 BC or a century or two later, towards the start of the so-called Early Dynastic period. It is arguable whether the disaster was man-made, since rivers in the flood-plains were always liable to migrate into easier channels, and changing sea-levels had effects upstream, but human activity may

34 *Floods can arrive very suddenly in Mesopotamia. Here water has filled what is usually a dry river-bed beside the rampart of Tell al-Rimah in the north. Rivers like this may have been perennial in prehistory.*

have tipped the balance. What happened, more or less abruptly, is that the main course of the Euphrates shifted, to the delight of some people but much to the embarrassment of those who had lived beside the old channels. So those who had controlled ample supplies of water found that there was no longer enough to support themselves in the style to which they had become accustomed. This is the first recognizable instance of disintegration in south Mesopotamian culture. There were plenty of people who were in a position to maintain traditions of civilized life inherited from the Uruk period, but rural and urban settlement accommodated itself generally to a new geographical pattern. If there was any one flood which gave rise to the legend of Atrahasis, it is likely to have occurred during this period of instability.

The picture which slowly emerges, over centuries, is one of local centres competing for access to water and irrigable land. In fact it can be argued that much the most efficient method of water use in south Mesopotamia is based on small-scale, locally organized operations. This is the system that has repeatedly emerged, throughout history, after more grandiose schemes have been buried under accretions of salt and silt. Small-scale work ensures local knowledge without the obligation to contribute to the support of external institutions and is least likely to result in over-exploitation of the land, salinity, and declining yields. Yet small-scale operations still provoke competition and conflict between people on different stretches of a watercourse, with those who are located upstream, and therefore have prior access to water, tending to gain the upper hand. The results of this process can be discerned through the periods known as Early Dynastic II and III (2600-2200 BC). The population became concentrated in a diminishing number of fortified centres, and it is entirely appropriate that one of the earliest political disputes to feature in historical records turns out to be concerned with land and water.

The city states of Umma and Lagash lay not far from one another in southeastern Mesopotamia, close to the region where waters from the Euphrates and the Tigris merged. The location of the border between the two states was a constant source of friction. It seems to have been settled by arbitration around 2400 BC, with a monument erected to mark the frontier, but our primary record, which comes from Lagash, states that the ruler of Umma had removed the marker and occupied the disputed territory. Around 2300 BC a resurgent Lagash took the territory back and re-established a new set of markers, together with the old one, along a boundary canal. It seems that the disputed land was still farmed by people owing allegiance to Umma, but they were obliged to pay tax to Lagash. Then the next generation fought the war again. Naturally it was the ruler of Umma who took the initiative, and destroyed, as best he could, the structures marking the boundary. After another victory for Lagash, the situation was complicated by the intervention of the ruler of Zabalam, further upstream, who obtained control of Umma and took over the old claim against Lagash. At this point there seems to have been renewed arbitration, with a compromise solution.

35 *Stone wall plaque of Enannatumi, ruler of Lagash, about 2300 BC. From Girsu.*

One of the intriguing features of this account is the availability of independent arbitration. The arbitrator is named as the ruler of Kish, a city in the northern part of the alluvial plain. A number of Mesopotamian rulers were to claim this title, Great King as it were, as if it implied the general leadership of the Sumerian world, and it is likely that at some time before, say, 2500 BC, the king of Kish did exercise a serious hegemony, with powers of arbitration as well as cultic duties. Many centuries later, a scheme was devised to legitimize Sumerian

36 *Sumerian chariot charging. From the Standard of Ur. About 2400 BC.*

kingship as a divine award, and it was thought then that the dynasty of Kish had been the first to hold power after the flood. There is valid historical information behind this story, since one of the last rulers of the Kish dynasty was named En-mebaragesi, and this very name, with the title King of Kish, was written on a stone bowl that has emerged from excavation. The son of En-mebaragesi, moreover, in another late story that has earlier antecedents, is recorded as marching from Kish to demand the allegiance of the city of Uruk, where he was confronted by an upstart named Gilgamesh, the hero of the most famous of all Mesopotamian myths. Evidently we are still some steps short of genuine political history, but the textual references to warfare combined with archaeological evidence from cities and defensive walls offer a convincing impression of internecine ferocity in south Mesopotamia.

Yet, concurrent with these accounts, there are traces of a greater unity inherited from prehistory. This is both ideological and material. The situation in Early Dynastic Sumer is thus comparable with other historical ages when independent city states, as in Classical Greece or Renaissance Italy, combined dynamic political rivalries with shared enthusiasms for technical innovation and intellectual adventure. If the process of invention in Sumer is not overt, the results are nonetheless startling.

Ideological unity is partly expressed through religion. The principal Sumerian gods were natural forces, personified in the gods of particular cities. Obviously there were innumerable divine forces and inherited rituals, and gods had a range of characteristics reflecting complex origins, but by about 2400 BC, and probably much earlier, there had developed a recognized Sumerian pantheon. There was also a tradition that the gods

37 Left *Stone wall plaque showing a naked priest, followed by three worshippers, pouring an offering in front of a seated god. Below, more worshippers carry animal offerings, while the priest's libation is poured on to a potted plant in front of a temple building. From Ur. About 2300* BC.

38 Below left *Votive statue of a man: the nose was attached separately or repaired later. About 2400* BC.

39 Below *Votive statue of a woman. Stone statues like this, dedicated in temples, demonstrated devotion to the gods, and some give the name of the donor. Many caches of them have been found, hidden away after the donors had died. About 2200* BC.

40 *Man's head, originally inlaid, from a votive statue. From Sippar. About 2300* BC.

met at the city of Nippur in the heart of south Mesopotamia, and there discussed matters of common interest such as the flood. In particular, it was at Nippur that the assembly of gods decided which Sumerian city was to have hegemony, and for how long. The principal kings took good care to contribute to the maintenance of religious buildings at Nippur.

Since there is no suggestion that Nippur owed its religious prestige to military power, it has been proposed that its status goes back to a period, closer to 3000 BC, when the Sumerian communities of south Mesopotamia were grouped together in a religious or political league. The proposal is supported by the discovery, at several Sumerian sites, of groups of clay sealings from packaged goods on which are written the names of widely separated cities. These sealings imply close cooperation between cities towards the start of the Early Dynastic period, even the existence of some kind of corporate property. Circumstances leading to the creation of such a league might have been the perception of an external threat, human or environmental, or simply a common persuasion.

The method by which the gods reached their decisions, essentially open discussion weighted by the opinions of the senior individuals present, also offers a model of Sumerian government. This is not inconsistent with the eventual presence of kings and dynasties, but suggests a background from which they may have emerged. Here the account of Gilgamesh and the king of Kish is instructive; though written down much later, as legend rather than history, it shows one way in which human decisions might be taken. In summary, Gilgamesh is king of Uruk, but he consults two separate bodies of citizens, one consisting of older and the other of younger men, over whether or not to resist the king of Kish.

What probably happened is that, in all Mesopotamian communities, power originally depended on family, property and personality, much as it tends to do elsewhere. In some circumstances it became necessary to choose someone who could act for the whole community, as military leader or administrator. The Sumerian words for ruler depend upon local circumstances; one standard term means effectively 'chief', and can be applied as readily to a chief workman as to a chief warrior. A temporary appointment, however, is sometimes liable to become permanent. The need for capable people to be war leaders, to take responsibility for public works such as irrigation, and to control temple institutions and their income, were all factors which might tend to concentrate influence and power in determined or judicious hands.

While different cities in this period developed in broadly similar ways politically, with local variations, the material culture of Mesopotamia generally displays features that were to be characteristic of civilizations in the area for thousands of years to come.

The standard building material was mud, with an admixture of straw to bind it. The mudbricks were usually made to a regular shape with the help of a wooden frame, and dried hard in the sun. They were laid with mud mortar. Such bricks, unimpressive though they sound, have some excellent qualities in practice. They are cheap and universally available, they provide good insulation in a climate with uncomfortable extremes of temperature, and they can be incorporated in any structure just as reliably as can baked brick or stone. The one requirement is that they should be protected from rain and damp. This can largely be achieved by mud-plastering the wall faces, and ensuring that the plaster is properly maintained.

Other materials were used as well. If stone was available, it clearly made stronger foundations than mudbrick, while baked brick came to be used for features such as drains, open courtyards and exposed facades. Bitumen, which wells to the surface naturally in several places in Mesopotamia, was used to waterproof vulnerable points. The roofs were sometimes arched, but most commonly they consisted of layers of matting laid on beams and covered with a layer of compressed mud, again an adequate system given regular maintenance. Besides the permanent structures, there were reed huts, and tents that can seldom have left significant traces in the ground.

With these materials, the people of Mesopotamia constructed town walls and fortresses, public and private buildings, that were comparable to those of any other civilization. The one problem is that mudbrick loses its cohesion when buried, so that excavated buildings cannot be resurrected as they originally stood, and they fail to attract admirers.

The towns in which these buildings stood varied widely, if we may judge from snap impressions gained from sites of diverse periods, but they have significant features in common. First, there is no overall ground-plan, even in freshly founded settlements. Any particular building or defensive wall may clearly have been designed as a unit, but the conglomeration of buildings which house the people and their industries is the product of erratic growth. Thus at Tell Taya, for instance, a town of the late Early Dynastic or Akkadian period in north Mesopotamia, domestic buildings conform to a grid pattern here and there, but this results from following natural contours and from development along sensible routes, not from wholesale imposition of standard rules. Similarly, building units vary hugely in size. This manifestly reflects the diversity of social status and the varying control of resources exercised by families and institutions within the community. Some buildings qualify as palaces, and somewhere there will have been the residence of the individual, almost certainly a man, having the greatest nominal power; but other large domestic buildings represent checks and balances within the organization of society. Industrial activities are scattered

41 *Mudbricks drying in the sun with a demonstration in the foreground showing how they are laid. These bricks, flat on one side and rounded on the other, are not unlike the Sumerian plano-convex bricks, and were still being made in a village near Mandali, north-east of Eshnunna, about AD 1966.*

42 *Part of a typical Mesopotamian town-plan (Tell Taya, about 2200 BC) showing how practical considerations, such as the existence of roads and opportunities to expand, distorted the usual preference for rectilinear house-plans.*

throughout the town. Basic industries attested, at one Mesopotamian town or another, include the production of leather and textiles, the working of tools and weapons from copper, bronze, or occasionally still flint, the manufacture of pottery, and the preparation of luxury goods. Always the most important, however, was the provision of food, stabling and storehouses.

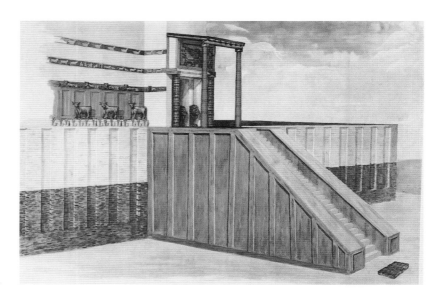

43 *Proposed reconstruction of the facade of the temple-tower or ziggurat at Tell al-'Ubaid, with the temple of the fertility goddess Ninhursag on top. About 2300 BC.*

Throughout these towns there were temples, religious shrines modelled ultimately on human houses where gods could reside. Many were small chapels at street corners, others attracted official patronage and qualify as good architecture. Much the grandest were the temples of the principal gods of each town or city. A temple, moreover, represented not merely a god's house but a god's household, and might need to accommodate staff and store-rooms in addition to the divine occupant. In south Mesopotamia these temples carry on the tradition established by the high terraces of the Uruk period. The process was assisted by the understanding, which developed in the south, that particular gods such as Nanna or Sin, the Moon god, resided in a particular city, in this case Ur, and that this city corresponded to his personal estate. He conferred favour on the local ruler and received magnificent structures in return, though he also shared in the city's discomfiture when enemies threatened. So the major cities of south Mesopotamia acquired a temple-tower or ziggurat apiece.

At a more technical level, there were many differences in the material culture of Early Dynastic Mesopotamia, primarily between north and south. These are expressed

44 Above right *Stone statue of Kurlil, an official in the city of Uruk, who was responsible for some of the construction work at Tell al-'Ubaid. About 2300 BC.*

45 *Copper relief of a lion-headed bird holding two deer, which may have been placed above the entrance of the Ninhursag temple at Tell al'-Ubaid. About 2300 BC.*

46 Opposite *Jar of the distinctive Ninevite 5 painted pottery, used in north Mesopotamia about 2600-2500 BC. From Nineveh.*

47 Left *Jar of incised Ninevite 5 pottery. From Nineveh. About 2400 bc.*

by the development in the north of a kind of craft pottery, known as Ninevite 5, with painted and incised varieties, which is a world away from the mass-produced vessels of the south. There is greater uniformity within south Mesopotamia, but also some regional distinctions between its northern half, Akkad, and its southern half, Sumer. These names correspond to an emergent linguistic division, in that the Sumerian language remained preponderant in the south whereas Akkadian, a Semitic language, was becoming more and more important in the north. This development resulted almost certainly from the presence of pastoral people, speaking Akkadian or related dialects, who occupied the fringes of the settled land and were available to take habitable space that fell vacant. It is a process of infiltration, sometimes but by no means necessarily hostile, that is well attested throughout Mesopotamian history, leading ultimately to the supremacy of Arabic. The presence of Akkadian speakers in Early Dynastic Mesopotamia is certain from the appearance of the language in documents, but individual Akkadians are not readily distinguishable from Sumerians. It has sometimes been maintained that there was conflict between them, as there often has been between pastoralists and arable farmers. There has to be this possibility, since the social and religious structures of people speaking distinct languages are not likely to coincide, but the evidence at this stage is uncompelling, and names in both languages can appear within single families.

An intriguing example of south Mesopotamian uniformity is the employment of a particular kind of mudbrick, known as plano-convex because it is flat on one side and convex on the other. Mudbricks of this idiosyncratic shape have been found throughout the region and were once treated as diagnostic of the Early Dynastic period, though we now know that they lasted somewhat longer. The culture of south Mesopotamia in the Early Dynastic period, like that of the Uruk period beforehand, also influenced neighbouring regions. When Ebla, in central Syria, adopted a writing system based on Sumerian, this was a considerable westward expansion from the middle Euphrates, where the culture of Mari was aligned with that of south Mesopotamia. Mari has also produced, among much else, statues of a particular kind which, while best known from extensive excavations in the region near the Diyala river, is also familiar from the main Mesopotamian sites such as Nippur and Ur. These statues were votive, dedicated in shrines to commemorate the devotion of individual donors – a few of whom, after about 2400 BC, had their own names carved on them. Both men and women are represented, usually wearing what seem to be woollen clothes. Similar statues were dedicated at Ashur and even at Tell Chuera in the far north-west of Mesopotamia, and it is clear that long-distance contacts were renewed whenever circumstances allowed.

A Sumerian record of such contacts survives in a legend about a king of Uruk and the ruler of a country, Aratta, which lay somewhere beyond mountain ranges in eastern Iran. The king of Uruk required from Aratta, for the decoration of a Sumerian temple, goods which were unobtainable in Sumer: gold, silver, lapis lazuli and carnelian. In return Uruk could offer grain. These, at least, seem to be the essential elements of the transaction, once references to divine favour and ritual challenges have been stripped away. The emergence of a staple food as a traded commodity, if this interpretation is correct, is one of the most important developments in the ancient Middle East. It made possible the establishment of communities which exported luxury goods to Mesopotamia but were liable, like some modern colonial states, to be or become dependent on the trade for their own stability. Within Mesopotamia, meanwhile, there was an incessant demand for goods which trade alone might not be able to supply in adequate quantity.

The city of Ur, located close to the Gulf at the south-eastern extremity of Mesopotamia, has contributed the most abundant material evidence for Early Dynastic trade. This is the result of a practice, so far only attested at Ur, which has led to the preservation of traded goods in enormous quantities. It seems that at Ur, for a century around 2400 BC, some people of distinction took substantial retinues of attendants with them to the grave. These graves or 'death-pits' were full of objects made from imported metals and precious stones. There has been much discussion about the identity of the people buried in these so-called Royal Graves at Ur. The original supposition was that they were straightforward kings and queens. Parallels were drawn with practices in several other cultures, such as those of central Asia, where mass burials on the occasion of royal deaths have been recorded; it was even suggested that the Sumerians themselves had reached Mesopotamia from central Asia. Alternative explanations have been that the burials were connected with ritual sacrifices made to ensure fecundity or to avert ill luck. A slightly

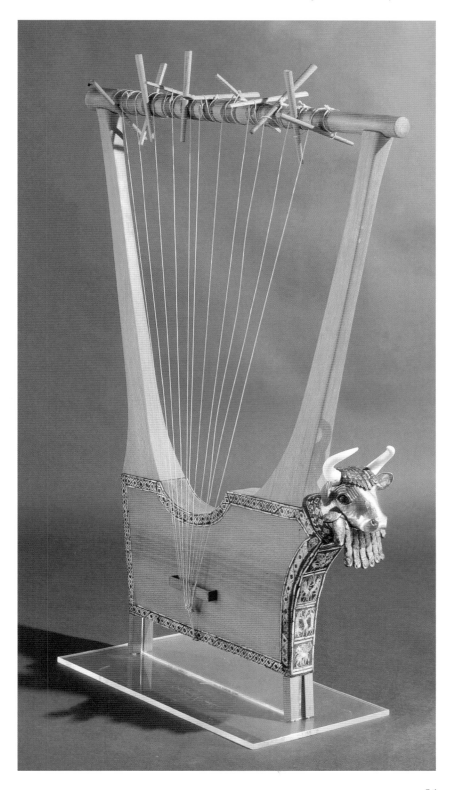

48 *Restored Sumerian lyre.*
From Ur. About 2400 BC.

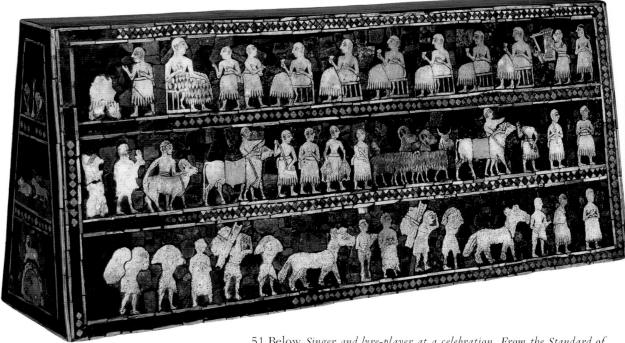

49 Above *The so-called Standard of Ur, an elaborately inlaid work of art, found crushed in a tomb at Ur. It has been restored, but its exact original shape and purpose are unknown. About 2400 BC*

50 Below *Sumerian ruler with attendant at a celebration party. From the Standard of Ur. About 2400 BC.*

51 Below *Singer and lyre-player at a celebration. From the Standard of Ur. About 2400 BC.*

52 Opposite left *Gold hair-rings, engraved fastener, and finger-ring with lapis lazuli inlay, worn by Pu-abi. From Ur. About 2400 BC.*

53 Opposite right *Shell containers for coloured cosmetics. From Ur. About 2400 BC.*

54 Opposite below *Gold and lapis lazuli amulets worn by Pu-abi. From Ur. About 2400 BC.*

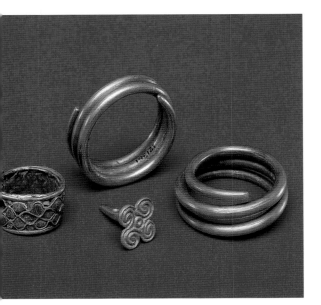

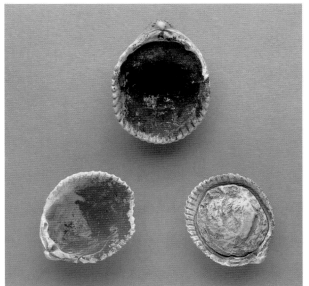

55 *Reconstruction by A. Forestier of the scene in one of the Ur graves, shortly before the participants in the ceremony took poison and were buried beside their dead lord.*

56 Left *Rein-ring of gold and silver. It was fixed on the pole of an ox-drawn sledge, with the reins passing through it (see fig.36). From Ur. About 2400 BC.*

57 Opposite I*nlaid statuette of a ram and a plant, probably used as a support. From Ur. About 2400 BC.*

different approach has been to see the burials as those of priest kings, given the close connections sometimes found between priesthood and kingship. The mass Early Dynastic graves would then be extreme instances of a kind of ritual which continued to be performed, on a more modest scale, for centuries to come, and which conformed to specific requirements of the cult at Ur. These graves have been disconcerting to scholars because of the difficulty of identifying related traditions in Sumerian legend, with doubts being cast on the best available parallel, an apparent reference to the mass death of family and retainers in a Gilgamesh legend. So the commonly fertile confrontation of archaeological finds with written

58 Previous pages *Selection of stone vessels – calcite, chlorite and marble – and one of gold from the tomb of Pu-abi, the 'Queen' at Ur. While some vessels found at Ur had been made locally from imported materials, most of the stone ones were made abroad and probably contained luxury products. A few were painted. About 2400 BC.*

evidence is for once frustrated, and the social implications remain obscure. What is evident is the abundance of imported goods at Ur.

Some items definitely came from the west of Mesopotamia, but most were from the east. The principal metal in the graves is copper; there were copper sources in Iran and Turkey, but some of the most abundant and best attested are in the Oman peninsula, at the entrance to the Gulf. Sumerian pottery has even been found there, and trace-element analysis has suggested an Omani source for at least some of the Ur copper. Gold and silver, also abundant in the graves, have not yet been traced to their sources, though they too could have been from the east. Stone vessels of chlorite and translucent calcite are again likely to have derived from the Gulf trade, most of them probably originating in Iran. The two kinds of stone used most frequently in the Ur jewellery, however, could have come from even further afield. Carnelian beads of exceptional quality are ascribed to a source in Gujerat in western India, while the nearest source of lapis lazuli, so far as we know, was in northern Afghanistan. In the Ur graves there was lavish use of these red and blue stones, interspersed with gold and silver, for both male and female jewellery.

59 *Pu-abi in the finery of death. This reconstruction is based on evidence from her tomb at Ur. About 2400 BC.*

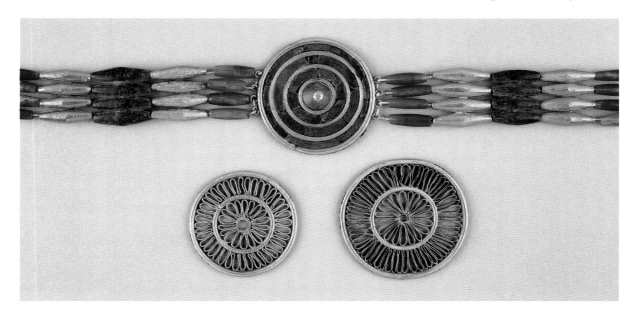

60 *Diadem of gold, carnelian and lapis lazuli, worn by a child about 2300 BC. From Ur.*

61 *Beads and pendants of gold, carnelian and lapis lazuli, from one of the Royal Graves at Ur. About 2400-2300 BC.*

62 *Inlaid board for the so-called Royal Game of Ur, with gaming pieces and four-sided dice. This was a race game for two players, based on the same principles as Ludo. It was known from the eastern Mediterranean to India. From Ur. About 2400* BC.

63 Opposite above *Carved stone with integral handle, possibly a weight made in Iran. From Ur. About 2400-2200* BC.

64 Opposite below *Inlaid decoration on a Sumerian lyre* (*see fig.48*). *About 2400* BC.

The prosperity of Ur has to be attributed largely to its position at the head of the Gulf, where it was one of the natural trading centres. Other trade undoubtedly passed overland, through Iran, where the great city of Susa dominated the plain west of Mesopotamia, besides having its own access to the sea. Sea trade had the advantages of speed and convenience. Any such trade, by land or sea, must have been subject to the vagaries of banditry, piracy and tax collection, but the Ur finds testify to the success that was possible in favourable circumstances.

While Ur had its own special situation, the other cities of Mesopotamia continued to compete for land and water in the manner recorded for Umma and Lagash. The Sumerian king-list suggests a sequence of dominant cities, first among equals, but the pattern may rather have been a growth in the degree of domination achieved. At the same time, within cities, there was a tendency for power to become centralized at the expense of individual freedom. That, at least, is what happened at Lagash, and we can postulate the same elsewhere.

The events in Lagash are recorded in documents left by a reforming king whose name, in current scholarship, is thought to have been

Uru-inim-gina. We cannot tell whether this man really instituted the reforms claimed by him, or whether they were an exercise in propaganda, benefiting one class only. What we can recognize is his acceptance of the concept of an ideal world, without oppressive government. According to Uru-inim-gina, he was faced on accession with a situation in which palace bureaucrats extorted goods from all and sundry, including the local god, and had extended royal ownership over much of the land. Uru-inim-gina claims to have eliminated these abuses, and to have succeeded in protecting the poor and needy from all kinds of extortion. In doing all this he was fulfilling the desires of his god and re-establishing, as best he could, a society imagined in later Sumerian tradition as a Golden Age, before the gods introduced pain and misery. Like many reformers, Uru-inim-gina eventually found the difficulties too much for him, and he fell victim to Lugal-zage-si, another hostile ruler of neighbouring Umma, who went on to conquer the whole of Sumer before being himself defeated by the first emperor, Sargon of Akkad.

Chapter Six | From estate to empire

Lugal-zage-si claimed to have marched from sea to sea, from the Gulf to the Mediterranean, expanding the horizons of Mesopotamian political power in a way not seen previously. He could hardly have done so, however, had the two seas not been linked already by a web of commercial relationships. Lugal-zage-si's march was probably a case of showing the flag. Under his successors, Sargon and Sargon's dynasty, lords of Akkad, there are references to campaigns down the Gulf, deep into Iran, through Syria, and up to the Turkish plateau. Not all the stories are necessarily authentic, but they have been periodically supplemented by archaeological finds, and offer a plausible outline of Akkadian interests. The conquests may have been facilitated by tribal contacts, as the Akkadian language of the emperors may well have been spoken in parts of north as well as south Mesopotamia, but the imperial campaigns seem almost indiscriminate, reaching out to bring all

65 *Stone bowl with two inscriptions. One states that it was brought to Mesopotamia as booty from Magan (probably Oman) by Naram-Sin of Akkad (c.2120-2084 BC), the other that it was dedicated to the Moon god Sin at Ur by the daughter of the later king Shulgi (c.2000-1953 BC). From Ur.*

foreign centres of prosperity and sources of raw materials into the Akkad universe.

The empire had its capital at Akkad, a city whose original location remains unknown though it was certainly in the northern part of south Mesopotamia, henceforth known as the land of Akkad; it was probably on a branch of the Euphrates north of Babylon. Sargon, the first Akkadian emperor (c.2200-2145 BC), is said to have been a man of obscure birth. Legend maintained that as a babe he was abandoned like Moses in a basket; rescued and adopted by a gardener, he grew to be royal cup-bearer at the court of Kish. He went on to become king in Akkad before defeating all the rulers both of the nearby cities and of the Sumerian south. Sargon's establishment of Akkad as capital city does suggest that his origins were unconventional by the standards of his

66 Top *Akkadian cylinder seal impression showing the brother of the king with two officials, followed by his secretary, Kalki, to whom the seal belonged. The armed guide and servants carrying equipment suggest a foreign expedition. About 2100 BC.*

67 Above *Akkadian cylinder seal impression showing various gods including the Sun god, who is cutting his way through the eastern mountains with a saw. About 2100 BC.*

68 *Copper head of an Akkadian king.*
From Nineveh. About 2100 BC.

Sumerian predecessors, since Akkad was not a long-established city; it owed its greatness, perhaps even its foundation, to Sargon alone. It may, for instance, have started life as an Akkadian tribal encampment. A tribal background would help account for the power and pertinacity of Sargon and his dynasty.

The land conquered by Sargon had for centuries been dominated by one city after another, with internal social and economic evolution in various directions, but without, so far as we can tell, any fundamental change in the assumptions around which life was built. Effectively the Sumerian homeland consisted of cities, each of which was the temporal estate of the city god, and significant portions of the city land belonged to temples. It has been calculated that, at Lagash, shortly before Sargon's arrival, the temples controlled between a quarter and a half of the city land, and a corresponding proportion of the population was in some way dependent on the temples. Since temple land was apparently inalienable, these institutions constituted a major element of stability in the state. Throughout the Early Dynastic period, as one city or another gained hegemony, gods gained or lost prestige with their cities, but they were not eliminated. Cities retained scope for independent action, with their ruling families and temple administrations intact.

The Akkadians, while leaving local power structures in place, did not accept this system; instead they created an empire. Sargon's grandson Naram-Sin (c.2120–2084 BC) has been credited with the main reforms, perhaps because he is the emperor about whom we are best informed. Essentially, the local rulers under him were transformed into governors answerable directly to him rather than to the city god. Akkad was then not just a city, holding temporary hegemony, but the centre to which all others had to look in much the same way as they had looked previously, without political connotations, to Nippur. The status of Akkad was reflected in the semi-divine status ascribed during his lifetime to Naram-Sin, symbolized in art by horns upon his head. So the emperor, as he may now be called, was the god towards whom the Sumerian cities, as parts of his estate, were required to direct their loyalty. All of south Mesopotamia could be regarded as the temple estate of the quasi-divine emperor. Much of north Mesopotamia too came under Akkadian control, but the details of administration are unknown; part of Elam, in south Iran, was also controlled by the Akkadians.

In the south the administration itself appropriately followed bureaucratic procedures which had originated in the temple estates, with heavy emphasis on accountability. There was a drastic change, however, with the imposition of consistent standards: standard weights, a standard script, and above all a standard language, Akkadian, to replace Sumerian in south Mesopotamia and Elamite in Iran. An art style of unprecedented vigour and imagination celebrated the unity and confidence of the empire, and public monuments proclaimed imperial invincibility.

The developments were resented. Again and again, with each new emperor, legend tells of massive Sumerian uprisings and the painful reassertion of authority. The deification of Naram-Sin, in particular, coupled with his casual attitude to the duties of a Great King, led to his

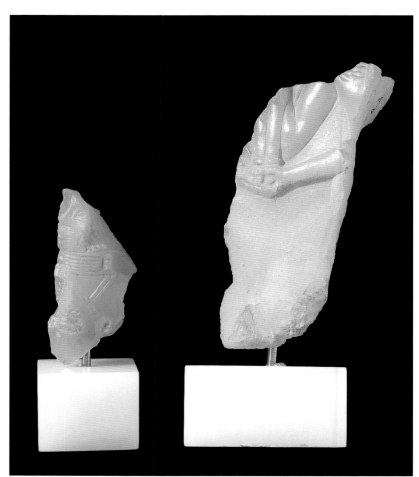

69 *Stela fragments showing the arms of a tribute-bearer and a woman with a high choker round her neck. The exceptional quality of the carving suggests a date in the reign of Naram-Sin (about 2120-2084 BC) when carved victory monuments were erected in many cities of the Akkadian empire. From Eridu.*

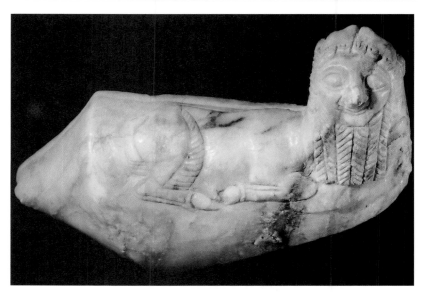

70 *Stone bowl possibly used for libations, in the shape of a shell decorated with a human-headed bull. From Ur. About 2200 BC.*

being accused of atrocious impiety. Yet the relative resilience of the empire shows it to have been a more effective political entity than the city states which resisted it. What it could not achieve, in the long term, was the retention of remoter conquests.

The eventual collapse of the Akkadian empire is ascribed to enemies from the barbaric fringes of Mesopotamia. The main people concerned, Gutians from the mountains of the north-east, are bitterly condemned by later Mesopotamian writers. In practice, the story is commonplace, one version of something that has happened in many parts of the world. A civilized area, in this instance south Mesopotamia under the Akkadians, attracts the attention and envy of rough neighbours. Wherever there is weakness, there is someone waiting to exploit it. As often, the precise causes of weakness are arguable – over-ambitious military adventures or overtaxing of the agricultural base, over-reliance on supporters of doubtful loyalty or the kind of ideological frailty implied by the failure of Naram-Sin's son to insist on a divine identity for himself too. In any event north Mesopotamia went its own way, while the south was overrun by the Gutian mountaineers. The kings of Akkad survived as local rulers, as did some governors of Sumerian cities, but the unity seemed to have gone.

Nonetheless this was an unnatural interruption. The length of time during which the Gutians were politically significant is unknown; they left few written records. In the absence of a centralizing power in Akkad, a centralizing Sumerian power emerged. The town of Girsu, by Lagash, which had been an Akkadian provincial centre, became the centre of a dynasty that seems to have flourished, in the so-called Gutian period, as if the Gutians had never existed. Its most celebrated ruler, Gudea (about 2030 BC, or perhaps a generation later), claimed to have campaigned into Iran, but most of his inscriptions refer to his pious works. These included the fetching of timber from the Mediterranean and stone from the Gulf as part of the reconstruction of a shrine. If we

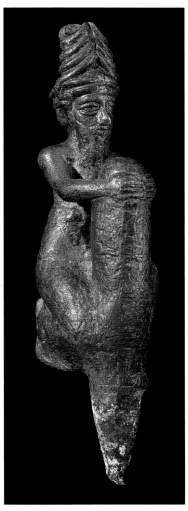

71 Above *Copper figurine of a god. These figurines were placed in the foundations of buildings, with elaborate ritual, to commemorate a ruler's piety and devotion. From Girsu. Reign of Gudea (about 2030 BC).*

72 *Stone duck weight. Weights were frequently made in the shape of ducks. This one has been officially inscribed with the ruler's name, while its weight, just over 60 kg, is given as two talents. Reign of Ur-Ningirsu of Lagash (about 2000 BC).*

73 *Torso of a diorite statue, with an inscription naming Gudea (about c.2030 BC). From Tell Hammam, near Umma.*

74 Above right *Woman's head, probably from a statue once dedicated in a temple. From Ur. About 2000 BC.*

are inclined to doubt these assertions, we have to confront the massive diorite statues that Gudea dedicated at Girsu, using stone that must have arrived by sea. It seems that, whatever the Gutians did, they could not prevent the persistent revival of commercial traffic. At the same time Girsu was a stronghold of the scribal tradition, expressed in hymns praising the king that have come to be regarded as supreme classics of Sumerian literature.

Oddly enough it was a king of Uruk, not Girsu, who is credited with expelling the Gutians from south Mesopotamia. This man, Utu-hegal, about 2020 BC, may simply have been clearing the land of bandits who no longer had much incentive to stay, but legend has preserved a fine account of a week of dramatic victory. Far more important, probably, was Utu-hegal's interest in reconstructing and maintaining the irrigation systems on which Sumer had come to depend, the control of which lay at the root of power in the alluvial land. Like the Early Dynastic kings of Lagash, the Gudea dynasty regarded the upkeep of canals as a fundamental royal responsibility, and one of the few further pieces of information we are given about Utu-hegal, besides his expulsion of the

Gutians, is that he was drowned while inspecting a dam.

The real successors of the Akkadian emperors were the emperors of the so-called Third Dynasty of Ur. The first of them, Ur-Nammu (about 2018-2001 BC), had been governor of Ur under Utu-hegal. He founded a dynasty which lasted about a century, and re-established the unity of south Mesopotamia, this time under nominally Sumerian control. If we may judge from what records survive, there was an ideological chasm between the imperial propaganda of Akkad and of Ur. The militant triumphalism of the former is contrasted, at Ur, with something approaching reticence. Ur monuments commemorate piety, not pillage. Yet, from the names assigned to years, on which we rely for some framework of imperial history in this period, there were many campaigns into north Mesopotamia and Iran. Ur certainly came to control parts of Iran in addition to south Mesopotamia itself. Moreover, if its conquests were more modest than those of Akkad, its methods of unifying the empire were no less thorough.

Once again a Sumerian was posing as Great King, performing cultic duties in a domain of divine estates. At the same time he was in fact supreme ruler, appointing governors and controlling, through his officials, the entire network of canals and communications which held the land together.

75 Below *Proposed reconstruction of the temple-tower or ziggurat of the Moon god at Ur, as built by Ur-Nammu (about 2018-2001 BC), founder of the Neo-Sumerian Third Dynasty of Ur.*

76 Above *Shulgi (about 2000-1953 BC) used baked bricks to construct what was probably his own dynastic mausoleum at Ur. This view, from one of the tomb chambers, was taken during the excavations about 1930.*

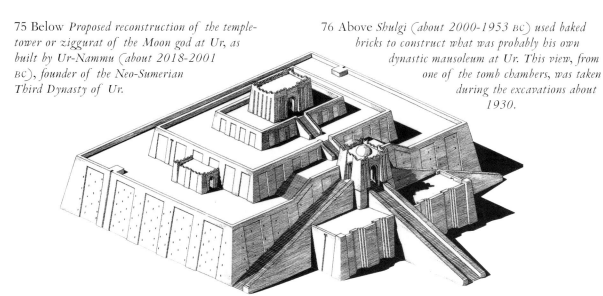

77 *Beads from Akkadian or later graves at Ur: the agate, the carnelians etched with white patterns, and the green bloodstone beads were probably all imported to Mesopotamia from India. About 2100-2000 BC.*

So it was logical that he should, like his Akkadian predecessors, acquire divine status. This development may have been implicit in the reign of Ur-Nammu, but again it was a later king of the dynasty, as once Naram-Sin so now Shulgi (2000-1953 BC), who took the matter to its logical conclusion and became a god in person.

Ur-Nammu has left many records of his achievements, most notably the great ziggurat that still stands at Ur, one of several which he reconstructed. He also encouraged a revival of foreign trade, renovating a harbour at Ur for the import of copper and other goods from the Gulf, paid for with goods such as textiles and with silver from the north. It is halfway through the reign of Shulgi, a man who ruled for almost half a century, that documentation of Ur administrative procedures becomes really abundant. It reveals a bureaucracy whose concern for detail is uncomfortably totalitarian, reflecting the efficiency of official methods of accountancy. At the same time there is evidence that the economy incorporated a substantial private sector whose records have not been satisfactorily preserved. The government and temple institutions included practitioners of all necessary crafts: there were workshops producing textiles and leather, carpentry and carved stone, metalwork and jewellery, and doubtless pottery too. The most prominent activities recorded, however, were the management of vast herds of cattle and sheep, and the production and processing of grain and other goods.

Meanwhile, outside south Mesopotamia, other states have left fewer written records of their existence. Ashur acquired an Ur governor at one stage; there were several campaigns by the Ur kings into the hills north-east of Mesopotamia. Mari was sometimes on friendly terms with Ur, but may have remained independent. In north Mesopotamia there were many large cities such as Tell Taya whose foundation went back to the end of the Early Dynastic period; some belonged to the kingdom of Urkish, under kings with Hurrian names. The extensive fertile plains of the north have never been subjected to the regular cycles of centralization and disintegration which the interdependent canal systems impose on the south, and the pattern of evolution is more erratic.

Uncivilized neighbours were responsible for the disintegration of the Ur empire as they had been for its Akkadian predecessor. On this occasion the developments can be followed more closely through authentic contemporary records. The people primarily concerned were the Amorites, yet more tribal pastoralists from the west, speaking dialects and languages related to Akkadian. This movement of pastoralists is so like that of the Aramaeans at a later date, of the Arabs later still, and of successive Arab tribes throughout historical times, all competing for territory on the northern fringes of Arabia and into Mesopotamia, that the appearance of the Amorites may most readily be interpreted in the same way. The contempt of the modern cultivator for the pastoralists on his doorstep echoes Sumerian complaints about the Amorites, who were ignorant of houses and tombs, cereals. and cooking: all the decencies of urban life. Yet these people, with flocks needing food, seeped unstoppably into the tidy Ur empire. A

78 Rock-crystal cylinder seal with a metal mount. The seal has been decorated, inside the perforation, with stripes of red and white paint. From Ur. About 2000 BC.

79 Painted plaster plaque
probably showing Ishtar,
goddess of fertility,
depicted as a woman with
elaborate body paint and
possibly some jewellery and
a loin-cloth. The area of
the right eye is worn
away, but the left eye is
covered by paint, as if she
is blindfold. From Ashur.
About 2200 BC.

cross-country wall built to keep them away was not so much a serious defence as a symptom of despair. Steady infiltration was a different kind of invasion to that of the Gutian mountaineers, but its effect was comparable.

The capital city of Ur, whose rulers had invested so heavily in the unity of south Mesopotamia, found itself dependent on the empire for survival. If the supply of taxes and provisions failed, Ur was driven to starvation. Enterprising provincial governors could fend for themselves, but prices in the capital rose stupendously, as contemporary records show. In the end Ur was captured and ravaged by some of the very people against whom its rulers had campaigned for so long: northerners including Gutians, and Elamites from Iran. The emperor disappeared into captivity. Once again south Mesopotamia became a land of independent cities and tribal groupings, competing for water and life.

80 *Faience beads from Tell Taya. The technique of glazing may have been invented in north-west Mesopotamia. It was particularly popular towards the end of the Uruk period and under the Akkadians, when the first faience vessels were made. About 2100 BC.*

Chapter Seven | The emergence of the individual

81 *On this terracotta cone Lipit-Ishtar, king of Isin (about 1838-1828 BC), records some of the classic duties of an Old Babylonian ruler: he established justice in the land (a reference to his code of laws), and he restored a city wall and cleared a water channel. Probably from Ur.*

The dominance of the state institutions, which seems to run through early Mesopotamian history, reflects in part the nature of our sources rather than the reality. There are many allusions to the activities of people outside the state system, not directly linked to temple or royal palace, but they happen to be poorly documented before about 1900 BC. In the Old Babylonian period which followed, the position is reversed–and private individuals become more accessible. Yet there is also a sense in which Mesopotamia after 1900 BC was indeed a more open society, less liable to regimentation than previously.

This change is symbolized by the issuance of written collections of laws, and by the nature of their content. Typically, this was not any sudden innovation but grew out of preceding practice. Uru-inimgina had already displayed an interest in the righting of wrongs, though his efforts may have been selective rather than aimed at the protection of society in general. Ur-Nammu claimed to have established justice, and some of his written laws survive. Yet it is in the centuries following the destruction of Ur-Nammu's dynasty that there developed, at least in south Mesopotamia, an insistence among rulers that they were not just divinely chosen for kingship but that they ruled equitably, and that private citizens could flourish under the protection of the rule of law.

The term 'law', though generally used, is a little misleading. What we have are legal rulings, recording what seemed fair and reasonable by reference to specific judgements. Collections of these rulings from different cities have much in common. The only complete collection is that inscribed on a stone monument of Hammurapi, king of Babylon (1696-1654 BC), and it covers a great range of subjects. They include the hire of boats, the duties of tenant farmers, family law, inheritance, apprenticeship, manslaughter, perjury, and much more. The collection points to the king's responsibilities as final arbiter, but is a world away from the formality of most royal inscriptions. This deals instead with a ragbag of real individuals, whose rights and obligations depend on age, sex and social status.

Some rulings maintain the antique deterrent concept of 'an eye for an eye'; this is likely to have been an Amorite introduction, the law of the desert, since monetary compensation was already established in Akkadian law. One example, exploring the notion of criminal negligence, is that of the surgeon condemned to lose his hands after an unsuccessful operation, although it is difficult to believe that this kind of penalty can really have been exacted of a doctor except in most peculiar circumstances. More comprehensible is the retribution imposed on a negligent builder responsible for the death of a client's son; his own son is to be killed. Concurrently, other rulings consider motives and make allowances for accidents: an owner is not responsible for damage caused by his ox unless he has had reason to suppose it dangerous. Generally, criminal behaviour is liable to severe punishments such as enslavement, physical mutilation and death. Monetary restitution is standard in civil cases.

Many of the rulings deal with economic affairs and the regulation of business. Furthermore, ancient Mesopotamia seems to have experienced the familiar phenomenon that, in free market conditions, the rich tend to become richer and the poor poorer. An effect of this is the accumulation of debts: the classic process involves the farmer repeatedly obliged by inadequate harvests either to eat the seed corn put away for following years, or to pay more than he can afford in taxes; he then borrows more corn, at interest, and eventually finds himself and his family indebted beyond redemption. Some Mesopotamian rulers cancelled such indebtedness, presumably for the sake of social and economic stability; these political decisions were counted as acts of justice, together with edicts asserting the prices of staple goods and services. It was one of the most ostentatious ways in which a king could help the individual people entrusted to his care.

Many archives of cuneiform tablets demonstrate the careful and systematic way in which private affairs such as marriages and transfers of property were recorded, at least among the more prosperous members of society. Transactions were completed in the presence of several witnesses, and cylinder seals validated the documents. The great majority of these seals were made to a basic design, which had become common

82 *Impression of the cylinder seal of a governor under Ur-Nammu. The scene, showing a man led into the presence of a god, is a fine version of one which became commonplace on late Neo-Sumerian and Old Babylonian seals. About 2000BC.*

under the Third Dynasty of Ur, and which incorporated a panel giving the name of the owner of the seal; an official might have several seals, bearing his name, for issue to subordinates. There is a great contrast here with the Early Dynastic situation, when seals of particular types seem to be associated with men or women but remain, for the most part, as anonymous as the majority of votive statues which individuals dedicated in shrines. Seal inscriptions had become more common under the Akkadians, but it was only after 2000 BC that they became normal.

The freedom and enterprise of Old Babylonian businessmen is amply attested. Mesopotamia remained, as it had long been, at the centre of a commercial network linking Turkey, Iran, Arabia, the Mediterranean and the Gulf, but it is now possible to identify some of the principal operators, male and cloistered female, who provided capital for caravans and ships. The pattern of operations varied. An example of a working system is provided by the voluminous records of Kanesh, a Mesopotamian colony located in central Turkey.

This colony consisted of people from Ashur, active for three generations or so around 1800 BC. It occupied one section of a town, managing its own affairs under the eye of the local king. Kanesh was only one of several colonies, with caravans continually passing to and fro on the perilous roads between them. Its own speciality was the import of tin and textiles from Ashur; silver and occasionally gold was received in exchange. Members of the colony also traded locally. The tin itself was imported to Ashur from the direction of Iran, so the Assyrians were middlemen in this trade. Some of the textiles originated in south Mesopotamia, but the majority were made at Ashur; the manufacture was often controlled by women whose husbands worked in Turkey, where they sometimes kept a second family. The local ruler and the authorities at Ashur took a close interest in the colony as a source of revenue, and the king of Ashur boasted of promoting trade. He, however, while occupying a special hereditary position as high priest of the god Ashur, was far from being a supreme ruler; one or more assemblies represented the chief families of the city, and there were other state officials and influential committees. The situation was one in which individuals were continually taking decisions for themselves rather than merely acting on behalf of the state.

Ashur seems to have retained, in this period, a pattern of government not dissimilar to that envisaged as prevalent when kingship was first emerging in the city states of south Mesopotamia. Had it not been for the Kanesh archive, the status of the Assyrian king might have been deduced from his own inscriptions and would have seemed more impressive. Other cities about which we are well informed, for the period after the disappearance of the Third Dynasty, include Ur itself, and there again private enterprise was thriving, without being directly dependent on royal support; the temple too was far less prominent than it had been among sources of capital for the Gulf trade. The rulers of what were now

83 Opposite *Painted terracotta statue of a woman, probably dedicated in a south Mesopotamian temple about 1800 BC.*

84 Below *Terracotta plaque of a travelling entertainer with monkeys, one of whom is playing a pipe. From Ur. About 1800 BC.*

85 *A distinctive kind of painted pottery, with ample use of stripes, was used in the Hurrian regions of northern Mesopotamia between 1900 and 1600 BC. Known as Khabur ware, after the name of the river in east Syria near which it was first identified, this pottery was also used in north-west Iran. From Chagar Bazar. About 1700 BC.*

86 Opposite *This copper peg, showing a figure with a basket of earth on its head, was made for burial in the foundations of a temple at Uruk. It dates from the reign of Ur-Nammu (about 2018-2001 BC). Similar pegs were still being made for Rim-Sin I of Larsa (about 1726-1667 BC).*

the main southern cities, Isin and Larsa, presented themselves as appointed by divine favour, according to the old rules, but society had changed. In effect, the temples which had acted as centres around which communities had coalesced, in daily life and in emergency, to divide irrigation water or defend against flood, had failed to cope with the problems of the third millennium and so had lost the ideological basis for their existence. They were even turning into private corporations: individuals inheriting anachronistic priestly duties, which entitled them to a share of the temple income, were beginning to find that what they had was a marketable investment. Against this background, political leaders mattered more than high priests, and even strong leaders such as the Third Dynasty rulers, who supported the temple system as an age-old bulwark of social stability, were unable to breathe independent life into it. The real centres had moved elsewhere; if one excavates an Old Babylonian town, the temple may have the finest architecture, under royal patronage, and there is probably a town council somewhere, but it is the palace that contains the archives documenting the serious exercise of power.

Geographically, too, the centre of power had moved, since the Third Dynasty was replaced by a hotchpotch of Amorite tribal leaders, the north-eastern representatives of a people which dominated the desert areas from the Gulf to the Mediterranean. They had been invading and infiltrating south and central Mesopotamia continuously for centuries, and they brought with them their own competitive brand of thought. Similarly, in north Mesopotamia, people with Hurrian names were establishing themselves in many small states, while the eastern fringes of Mesopotamia were open to Elamite settlement from Iran. Our sources, exemplified in a long series of archives from Mari, show all these people in an endless round of intrigue and warfare, with south Mesopotamia still highly important but no longer politically paramount.

If the old city state demanded the cooperative loyalty and obedience of its citizens, factors favouring desert survival included family solidarity and a willingness to take the initiative. So the Amorite rulers, not surprisingly, appear with individual strengths and weaknesses which affected the basis of government to a much greater extent than was feasible for a Sumerian king. For instance, one leader, Shamshi-Adad I, pulled the greater part of north Mesopotamia together into an empire under his control around 1700 BC, but its cohesion depended on his own imposing personality. On Shamshi-Adad's death, one of his sons immediately lost his inheritance, and the other only kept part of his with difficulty. This pattern was frequently repeated on a more modest scale. The Amorite rulers of Mari can often be seen governing on an ad hoc basis, torn between delegating substantial responsibility to subordinates and interfering personally in trivial decisions. Failure to delegate led to rigidity and incompetence, but if individuals showed too much initiative, there was trouble for the ruler. Officials were quite capable of transferring their loyalty; some of those at Mari did eventually opt for Hammurapi of Babylon. It was a volatile world.

When an institution is crumbling, there is usually another growing up underneath it. While the city temples of the gods of nature in south Mesopotamia were losing status, and human gods were proving themselves fallible, people as individuals still needed to reconcile themselves to the mysteries of life and death. Archaeologically, this need is partly reflected by the enormous number of terracotta figurines of gods, major and minor, which were made in the Old Babylonian period and were apparently used by individuals, outside the official palaces and shrines, for domestic worship. There is also a standard scene on the cylinder seal, alongside the owner's name, showing an individual introduced into the presence of a senior god by an intermediary, an intercessor. In texts, there is the emergence of an attitude whereby the ordinary human individual claims the right of direct communication with the divine: not merely with his personal god, or an intercessor, but with the higher forces which are held responsible for the vagaries of fate.

One symptom of this change, which like most changes in Mesopotamia cannot and should not be dated but has to be appreciated as developing over centuries, is the appearance and legitimation of

87 Stone statue of a woman worshipper. The paint on this statue is unusually well preserved. From Ur. About 1800 BC.

88 Copper statuette of the interceding goddess Lamma. From Ur. Probably about 1800 BC.

methods of magically predicting, through omens, the likely course of future events. There was a whole range of techniques, apparently based on the empirical study of what had actually happened after certain phenomena had been observed, and hence what was likely to happen again should the phenomena repeat themselves. The phenomena are varied: patterns of oil on water, flights of birds and much else, but one of the most valued was the pattern of markings on the livers of sacrificed sheep. These conveyed a message and brought the enquirer into immediate contact with supernatural powers, presided over by the all-seeing Sun god. It is characteristic of Shamshi-Adad's two heirs, however, that when one was faced with an alarming omen of this kind, the other firmly told him not to fuss. The pair were people acting for themselves, in character, not mere agents of divine authority.

This is free thought, which can lead anywhere. One letter records a sacrilegious theft of valuables from a shrine in terms suggesting that such a crime was unthinkable. Other minds explored, more constructively, the

movements of planets; agricultural methods; medicine, which could be practised with or without the help of magic; and mathematics, where the theorem of Pythagoras was proved a thousand years before the Greeks adopted, again from the east, the idea of alphabetic writing.

There is also philosophy. This interest is expressed in questions about the nature of divine justice in an unfair world, and appears also in the epic of Gilgamesh, which probably took shape as a single composition around this time. It is an evocative story, but there is one episode in particular which suggests a background of speculative thought. Gilgamesh, having lost his dearest friend, wishes to discover the secret of immortality known to the gods. He succeeds in locating a human being who has, in special circumstances, gained immortality. This man demonstrates to his visitor the power of sleep. As Gilgamesh sleeps, he is given a fresh loaf of bread each day; when he is finally awoken, there are seven loaves, in varying stages of staleness, lying beside him. With this lesson on the lesser enemy, Gilgamesh appreciates that death is inexorable; the

89 Above left *Terracotta plaque of a magical spirit with water flowing inexhaustibly from a vase. From Ur. About 1800* BC.

90 *Terracotta plaque showing an affectionate couple. From Ur. About 1800* BC.

91 Right *Painted terracotta statue of a seated god, possibly the Sun god Shamash who was responsible for omens. From Ur. About 1800* BC.

best he can do is leave a tangible memorial of himself in the magnificent walls of his city, Uruk. This story is the work of someone plainly dissatisfied with traditional explanations of man's place in the universe. It also includes, in advice offered to Gilgamesh by a wise woman he encounters on his way, the classic answer to all such worries: 'Eat, drink and be merry, for tomorrow we die!'

92 *Terracotta plaque showing a man and woman making love while the woman drinks beer through a straw. Informal scenes such as this, unlike monumental art, show the less public face of life in ancient Babylonia, but they may also have had some magical or religious significance. About 1700* BC.

93 Above *Illustrated tablet containing a set of geometrical problems. At this period the cuneiform script could still be read either from top to bottom or from left to right; soon afterwards the horizontal system prevailed. About 1800-1600* BC.

94 Left *Inscribed model of a sheep's liver, probably used for instructing pupils in divination. Each box describes the implications of a blemish appearing at that position. Probably from Sippar. About 1600* BC.

Chapter Eight | Epilogue

The rulers of the Third Dynasty of Ur (2018-1911 BC) took care to maintain and extend the canal system on which the agriculture and internal communications of their land depended. Many documents refer to management of the labourers hired or compelled to do this work. In the process potential problems were created, as the artificial straightening of a naturally meandering watercourse accelerates the flow and is liable to cause operational difficulties. Large-scale irrigation, moreover, unless carefully monitored, can easily lead to overexploitation and declining yields. These factors, and the discontent of an over-regulated workforce, may have contributed to the disintegration ostensibly caused by Amorite invasions.

The successor kingdoms based in Isin, Larsa, Babylon and elsewhere operated broadly the same canal system for a much longer period. Their greater efficiency may have resulted partly from the increased number of small family holdings of land, and partly from the absence of grandiose schemes. It was clearly a successful arrangement or it would not have lasted so long, and fine public buildings point to the material prosperity of south Mesopotamia, matching its intellectual sophistication. Some documents suggest a gradually widening economic gap between the rich and the poor, but this was the kind of problem that could be relieved by the cancellation of debts.

Warfare between the cities was not unusual, with shifting alliances reminiscent of the Early Dynastic period, and occasional intervention from outside south Mesopotamia. The result was similar too, in that the smaller states were gradually absorbed by their neighbours. Eventually, in the years following 1665 BC, Hammurapi of Babylon swept away his rivals and emerged as lord of an empire covering all of south Mesopotamia, and extending briefly to Mari and Nineveh.

An element in Hammurapi's success was good husbandry and consolidation of resources both by his predecessors and by himself in the early years of his reign, when canals and defences were constructed in the Babylon region. Hammurapi also attempted to revive the prosperity of areas he conquered in the old Sumerian heartland by work on a canal intended to serve all the great southern cities of the period: Nippur, Isin, Uruk, Larsa, Ur, and even Eridu. Less constructive was the method he employed in 1659 to defeat another important state, Eshnunna on the Diyala river; it was devastated by an artificial flood, and never seems to have recovered.

In 1645 Hammurapi's son, Samsuiluna, was faced with a rebellion of the southern cities. Two years later Ur and Larsa in the far south of his kingdom were virtually abandoned, while Nippur was experiencing severe difficulties over its water supply. This suggests that the Babylonian king had used his strategic upstream position to humble his adversaries by diverting the Euphrates water which would otherwise have reached them. The operation was successful, but the southernmost

95 *Hammurapi of Babylon (1696-1654 BC). The king has his right arm raised in worship.*

cities did not recover, while Nippur continued to experience difficulties for another ten years. It seems, then, that the diversion could not easily be reversed.

Then, in 1625, there was another rebellion in Nippur, and records from the city cease within a year; apparently its water had again been cut and the supply was not to be renewed for centuries. The rule of Hammurapi's dynasty was now restricted to an area round Babylon that was not much larger than Hammurapi had himself inherited. The difference is that Samsuiluna and his descendants ruled a kingdom sur-

rounded by areas of devastation instead of prosperous neighbours. In 1499 BC Hammurapi's dynasty disappeared.

If this interpretation of the evidence is correct, then Babylon brought disaster on itself by deliberately destroying the environment within which it had to live. It is an ironic commentary on the civilization responsible for an invention such as writing, generally seen as positive, that it should also offer such a prime example of human folly.

The world in which Hammurapi's descendants ruled a shrunken empire was one in which states of this size, centred on particular cities, were tending to lose political significance. Throughout the Middle East, a transformation was in progress.

At first the change was far from obvious. A dynasty of kings with Sumerian names ruled somewhere in the marshes between Babylon and the Gulf; there was a successor state to Mari on the Middle Euphrates. Yet in north Mesopotamia many cities seem to have been abandoned during the seventeenth century BC, and even the meticulous clerks of Ashur lost count of their kings. The immediate cause of the breakdown is obscure: as in prehistory, a long succession of bad harvests is a possible explanation, and one perhaps relevant to contemporary developments outside Mesopotamia itself. The end result, however, was the imposition of an entirely new order, in both north and south.

It had been foreshadowed by events such as the invasions to which the end of the Akkad empire was attributed. These movements of peoples were an unending process, as groups at all points of the compass competed for the vital resources of land and water, but in the centuries around 1600 BC Mesopotamia was not the only region affected. The southward movements of tribes which spoke Indo-European languages, and were probably capable of rapid travel with horses, destabilized all the northern borderlands of the Middle East, from Greece to India, and influenced areas where they themselves did not necessarily penetrate.

Written records of tribal migration are scarce, but its effect is plain. After 1500 BC, the people of Mesopotamia were once again ruled by newcomers. This time the aristocrats of the south were Kassites, with an empire extending deep into Iran where their homeland probably remained. In north Mesopotamia the Hurrian population acquired kings with Indo-European names. These men made war or peace, on equal terms, with the rulers of Elam, Egypt, and the newly established Hittite empire in Turkey; smaller city states were squeezed between them. Effectively, the horizons of international involvement had broadened beyond recognition.

As always, these newcomers were to be absorbed, disappearing from sight. Outside intrusions could not change the basic conditions of Mesopotamian existence. Agriculture was still practised. Trade and the economy could be revived. Enough literate people were left to maintain

96 *Tell al-'Ubaid temple column, about 2300 BC, made by coating a tree-trunk with coloured stones and shell. Such techniques, inherited from prehistory and using local rather than imported materials, disappeared with the collapse of Sumer.*

the intellectual traditions of the south, and to demonstrate their continuing vitality. In due course, over many centuries to come, Ashur and Babylon would recover, and grow to be capitals of empires far more extensive and centralized than those of Sargon and Shulgi.

These future developments, however, belong to the history of the whole Middle East, not of Mesopotamia alone. The achievements of the people of Mesopotamia were by then part of the common heritage of the ancient world, the essential groundwork of the civilization we all inhabit now.

Further reading

R.M. Adams, *Heartland of Cities* (Chicago 1981)

D. Collon, *First Impressions: Cylinder Seals in the Ancient Near East* (London 1987)

J. Curtis (ed.), *Early Mesopotamia and Iran: Contact and Conflict c.3500-1600 BC* (London 1993)

I.M. Diakonoff (ed.), *Ancient Mesopotamia: Socio-economic History* (Moscow 1969)

T.E. Downing and M. Gibson (eds), *Irrigation's Impact on Society* (Tucson 1974)

T. Jacobsen, *The Treasures of Darkness: A History of Mesopotamian Religion* (New Haven 1976)

S.N. Kramer, *The Sumerians* (Chicago 1963)

I.D. Levine and T.C. Young (eds), *Mountains and Lowlands: Essays in the Archaeology of Greater Mesopotamia* (Malibu 1977)

K.R. Nemet-Nejat, *Daily Life in Ancient Mesopotamia* (Westport/London 1998)

H.J. Nissen, *The Early History of the Ancient Near East 9000-2000 BC*, trans. by E. Lutzeier (Chicago 1988)

A.L. Oppenheim, *Ancient Mesopotamia: Portrait of a Dead Civilization* (revised edn, Chicago 1977)

S. Pollock, *Ancient Mesopotamia* (Cambridge 1999)

J.N. Postgate, *Early Mesopotamia: Society and Economy at the Dawn of History* (London/New York 1992)

M. Roaf, *Cultural Atlas of Mesopotamia and the Ancient Near East* (Oxford 1990)

H.W.F. Saggs, *Babylonians* (London 1995)

Chronology

The chronology of societies in the ancient Near East depends partly on documents such as Mesopotamian lists of kings and astronomical records; some of these are supported by contemporary Egyptian documents. Archaeological finds and sequences establish the general relationships of different regions and periods. This evidence, which varies greatly in quality, is supplemented by dendrochronology, which relies on tree-ring growth patterns in timber from ancient buildings. Annual variations in tree-ring size are sometimes affected by large volcanic eruptions, the exact dates of which can be determined from the presence of volcanic debris in arctic ice-cores; the evidence is scarce, because ancient timber seldom survives in good condition. The radiocarbon method of dating, which measures the decay of radioactive isotopes in organic remains, gives less exact results but is extremely valuable for dating societies which have not left written records.

Many events after about 900 BC can be dated precisely. For the period from 900 back to 1400 BC there may well be some cumulative error, but the maximum deviation does not exceed about twenty years. The dates for Assyrian and Babylonian rulers of 1400-500 BC are conveniently given by Brinkman (1977).

Further back in time, there is greater uncertainty. A period of over 500 years, ending with the fall of the First Dynasty of Babylon, is relatively well known (Edzard 1957) but its exact position in time is not established. Astronomical records may not be reliable. Documents naming Shamshi-Adad I of Assyria, however, a ruler whose approximate position within this period is known, have been found in a palace incorporating timber apparently cut in 1752 BC (Kuniholm et al 1996); this strongly suggests that Shamshi-Adad died after this year, and consequently that the widely quoted 'Middle Chronology', which dates the fall of Babylon to 1595 BC, should be replaced by a chronology which dates this event after 1570 BC. The latest date possible seems to be around 1500 BC. A case has been made for 1499 BC (Gasche et al 1998), and this minimum date, with others that depend on it, is used in this book.

The Third Dynasty of Ur will then have commenced about 2018 BC. The Akkadian empire probably disintegrated about 40 years earlier (Hallo 1971). If this is correct, the 56-year-long reign ascribed to Sargon, founder of the Akkadian empire, lasted from about 2200 to about 2145 BC. The preceding Early Dynastic II-III periods in Mesopotamia, which include the earliest known records of Sumerian kings (Cooper 1983: 19-20, 60; Ehrlich 1992: I, 103), may have lasted three or four centuries.

Dates assigned to other cultures for which no written records exist are based on radiocarbon and on archaeological comparisons, and many problems remain. Ehrlich (1992) presents the evidence region by region. Errors of several centuries become increasingly likely as one moves back in time, and it is often impossible to draw clear chronological distinctions between overlapping cultures and periods both inside and outside Mesopotamia.

References

BRINKMAN, J.A.
1977 Appendix: Mesopotamian chronology of the historical period. In A.L. Oppenheim, *Ancient Mesopotamia: Portrait of a Dead Civilization* (University of Chicago Press): 335-48. First edition 1964. Chicago/London (University of Chicago Press).

COOPER, J.S.
1983 *Reconstructing history from ancient sources: the Lagash-Umma border conflict* (Sources from the Ancient Near East 2/1). Malibu (Undena Publications).

EDZARD, D.O.
1957 *Die "Zweite Zwischenzeit" Babyloniens*. Wiesbaden (Harrassowitz).

EHRICH, R.W.
1992 Editor, *Chronologies in Old World Archaeology*. Third edition. 2 volumes. Chicago/London (University of Chicago Press).

GASCHE, H., J.A. ARMSTRONG, S.W. COLE, AND V.G. GURZADYAN
1998 *Dating the Fall of Babylon: a Reappraisal of Second-Millennium Chronology* (A Joint Ghent-Chicago Project) (Mesopotamian History and Environment, Series II, Mémoires IV). Ghent/Chicago (University of Gent, Oriental Institute of the University of Chicago).

HALLO, W.W.
1971 Gutium. *Reallexikon der Assyriologie und Vorderasiatischen Archäologie*, vol. 3 (9): 708-20. Berlin/New York (Walter de Gruyter).

KUNIHOLM, P.I., B. KROMER, S.W. MANNING, M. NEWTON, C.E. LATINI, AND M.J. BRUCE
1996 Anatolian tree rings and the absolute chronology of the eastern Mediterranean, 2220-718 BC. *Nature* 381 (27 June 1996): 780-3.

*c.*8000-6000
Early village settlements

*c.*6000-5500
Samarra culture in central and north Mesopotamia

*c.*5500-5000
Halaf culture in north Mesopotamia

*c.*5500-4000
Ubaid culture in south Mesopotamia, with expansion to north and west

*c.*4000-3500
Gawra culture in north Mesopotamia

*c.*4000-3000
Uruk culture in south Mesopotamia, with extension to north and west

*c.*3300-2500
Late Prehistoric period, including Late Uruk/Jamdat Nasr phase, Early Dynastic I-II, and early Ninevite 5

*c.*2500-2200
Early Dynastic III period

*c.*2450-2300
First Dynasty of Ur (including Pu-abi, Mese-ane-pada)

*c.*2380-2200
Rulers of Lagash (including Ur-Nanshe, Uru-inim-gina)

*c.*2200
Lugal-zage-si (ruler of Umma, Uruk and Sumer)

*c.*2200-2059
Akkadian Dynasty, including

*c.*2200-2145
Sargon

*c.*2144-2136
Rimush

*c.*2135-2121
Manishtushu

*c.*2120-2084
Naram-Sin

*c.*2083-2059
Shar-kali-sharri

*c.*2050-2000
Rulers of Lagash (including Gudea, Ur-Ningirsu)
Rulers of Uruk (including Utu-hegal)

*c.*2018-1911
Third Dynasty of Ur

*c.*2018-2001
Ur-Nammu

*c.*2000-1953
Shulgi

*c.*1952-1944
Amar-Sin

*c.*1943-1935
Shu-Sin

c.1934-1911
Ibbi-Sin

c.1921-1698
First Dynasty of Isin, including

c.1838-1828
Lipit-Ishtar

c.1930-1667
Larsa Dynasty, including

c.1739-1727
Warad-Sin

c.1726-1667
Rim-Sin

c.1798-1499
First Dynasty of Babylon

c.1798-1785
Samuabum

c.1784-1749
Summulael

c.1748-1735
Sabium

c.1734-1717
Apil-Sin

c.1716-1697
Sin-muballit

c.1696-1654
Hammurapi

c.1653-1616
Samsuiluna

c.1615-1588
Abi-eshuh

c.1587-1551
Ammiditana

c.1550-1530
Ammisaduqa

c.1529-1499
Samsuditana

List of illustrations with dimensions

H height   L length
W width   D diameter

The British Museum Photographic Service has provided photographs of objects in the British Museum Department of Western Asiatic Antiquities (WA), and particular thanks are due to Barbara Winter and Lisa Bliss for their skill, speed and patience in responding to our requests.

Contents page © S.N. Shaw Reade
1 Map drawn by Ann Searight
2 © J. E. Reade
3 WA 102081. H 13 cm
4 © J. E. Reade
5 WA 121201 (detail of Fig 49)
6 WA 133043. L 75 cm
7 WA 92989. H (of sheep) 10 cm
8 WA 121201 (detail of Fig 49)
9 WA 132092. H 9.5 cm
10 WA 121201 (detail of Fig 49)
11 Iraq Museum. H (of figures) 14 cm. From the Joint British Museum and University Museum (Philadelphia) excavations, 1923
12 WA 127814. L (of longest obsidian) 5.8 cm
13 Bowl: WA 1924-4-16,5. D 13.5 cm. Jar: WA 1924-4-16,7. H 10.3 cm
14 Left: WA 127582. D 15.7 cm; Right: WA 127585. D 14 cm
15 WA 127717. H 3.9 cm
16 WA 125381. H 7.4 cm
17 Left: WA 127706. H 5.4 cm. Right: WA 127707. H 4.8 cm
18 Left: WA 116894. H 4.3 cm; Right: WA 121002. H 4.2 cm
19 Leopards: WA 127616. W 12.1 cm. Snake: WA 127617. H 10.9 cm. Horns: WA 1934-2-10,262. H 6.2 cm
20 WA 122893. D 22.4 cm
21 WA 120000 (detail). H (of carved frieze) 16 cm. Presented to the British Museum by the National Art-Collections Fund
22 WA 122873. H 13.6 cm
23 WA 128840. H 6.5 cm
24 WA 138746. D 18 cm
25 WA 126475. H 5.7 cm
26 WA 134636. H 10.7 cm. Presented to the British Museum by E. Buck, Esq., 1965
27 WA 126397A. W 20.7 cm
28 WA 126460. H 13 cm
29 WA 116715, 120963, 120973, 126445, 126448. L (of leopard) 7.6 cm
30 Adapted from H.J. Nissen et al., Frühe Schrift und Techniken der Wirtschaftsverwaltung im alten Vorderen Orient (1990), p. 168, fig 17s
31 WA 140855. H 7 cm
32 WA 120850. H 7.5 cm
33 © J.E.Reade
34 © J.E.Reade
35 WA 130828. H 19 cm
36 WA 121201 (detail of Fig 49)
37 WA 118561. H 22 cm
38 WA 91667. H 14.8 cm
39 WA 116666. H 22.1 cm. Presented to the British Museum by the National Art-Collection Fund
40 WA 91877. H 11 cm
41 © J.E.Reade
42 © J.E.Reade
43 H.R.Hall and C.L.Woolley, Ur Excavations I, pl. 38
44 WA 114207. H 37.5 cm
45 WA 114308. L 288 cm
46 WA 1932-12-10,121. H 11.5 cm
47 WA 1932-12-12,38. H 11.5 cm
48 WA 121198A. H 112.5 cm
49 WA 121201. L 49.5 cm
50 WA 121201 (detail of Fig 49)
51 WA 121201 (detail of Fig 49)
52 WA 121361, 121372, 121378. D (of finger-ring) 2.1 cm
53 WA 139529, 139531, 139534. L (longest) 5.2 cm
54 WA 121404-7. H (of goat amulet) 3.2 cm
55 C.L.Woolley, Ur Excavations II, pl. 30
56 WA 121348. H 13.5 cm
57 WA 122200. H 45.7 cm
58 WA 121345, 121698, 121700-2, 121716, 121726. H (of cup) 9 cm
59 C.L.Woolley, Ur Excavations II, pl.128
60 WA 122206-8. D (of largest roundel) 4.9 cm
61 WA 121424-6. L (longer carnelian) 1.6 cm

62 WA 120834. L 30.1 cm

63 WA 91700. H 21 cm

64 WA 121198A (detail of Fig 48)

65 WA 118553. H 7.8 cm

66 WA 89137. H 3.4 cm

67 WA 89115. H 3.9 cm

68 Iraq Museum. H 36 cm. From the British Museum excavations, 1931

69 WA 114259-60. H 9.5 cm, 6 cm

70 WA 122254. L 14 cm

71 WA 102613. H 14.3 cm

72 WA 104724. L 49.5 cm

73 WA 92988. H 96 cm. Recovered by W.K.Loftus, 1850

74 WA 118564. H 8.3 cm

75 C.L.Woolley, Ur Excavations v, pl.86

76 C.L.Woolley, Ur Excavations vi, pl.12b

77 WA 120577, 120581, 120621, 120634-5, 122435, 122444. L (of agate with gold caps) 4.7 cm

78 WA 120529. H 5.3 cm

79 WA 118996. H 18 cm

80 © J.E.Reade, cf. WA 121418-23. L (longest bead) 3 cm

81 WA 114683. H 10.8 cm. Presented to the British Museum by Col. A.G.M.Hogg, 1920

82 WA 89126. H 5.3 cm. Presented to the British Museum by C.D.Cobham, Esq., 1880

83 WA 135680. H 40.2 cm

84 WA 116513. H 10.8 cm

85 WA 125351. H 22.8 cm

86 WA 113896. H 27.3 cm

87 WA 132101. H 15 cm

88 WA 123040. H 9.8 cm

89 WA 116813. H 13.4 cm

90 WA 116812. H 10.5 cm

91 WA 122934. W 13.3 cm

92 WA 116731. H 8.9 cm. Presented to the British Museum by Major Burn, 1925

93 WA 15285. H 26 cm

94 WA 92668. H 14.5 cm

95 WA 22454. H (above elbow) 15.5 cm

96 WA 115328, 116760. H 230 cm

Index

Italic text refers to illustrations

Akkad(ian), 45-9, 61-71, 74, 77, 86; *65, 69, 77, 80*
Al-'Ain, *26*
Amorite, 71, 74, 7-9, 84
Arab(ic), 49, 71, 77
Aramaeans, 71
Aratta, 50
Arpachiyah, 20; *12, 14, 15, 17, 19*
Ashur, 50, 71, 77, 86-7; *79*
Assyria, 6, 13
Athens, 6
Atrahasis, 38-40

Babylon(ia), 10, 13, 19, 63, 74, 79, 84, 86-7
Bau, *3*

Central Asia, 50
Chagar Bazar, *16, 85*
Chatal Huyuk, 17

Diyala, 50, 84

Early Dynastic period/culture, 40-61, 65, 68, 77, 84
Ebla, 50
Egypt, 6, 27, 86
Enannatum, *35*
Enki, 25,
En-mebaragesi, 42
Eridu, 25, 84; *69*
Eshnunna, 84; *41*
Euphrates, 6, 10, 13, 19, 24, 25, 29, 39-40, 50, 84
Europe, 6, 9

flood, 39-40, 44; *33, 34*

Gilgamesh, 42, 44, 54, 81-2
Girsu, 67-8; *3, 35, 71*
Greece, Greeks, 6, 42, 81, 86

Gudea, 67; *71, 73*
Gulf, 6, 28, 50, 67, 70, 77, 79, 86; *12*
Gutians, 67-9, 73

Habuba Kabira, 29
Halaf period/culture, 19-23, 27, 35; *12, 14, 16, 17, 19*
Hammurapi, 74, 79, 84-6; *95*
Hassuna period/culture, 18-9, 27
Herodotus, 6
Hittite empire, 86
Hurrian, 20, 71, 79, 86; *85*

India, 6, 86; *62, 77*
Indo-European, 86
Iran, 6, 17, 27-9, 34, 50, 58, 60, 62, 65, 69, 73, 77-9, 86; *63*
Iraq, 6, 10, 19-20, 27, 29
Ishtar, *79*
Isin, 78, 86; *81*

Jamdat Nasr, *26*
Jericho, 17

Kalki, *66*
Kanesh, 77
Kassites, 86
Khabur ware, *85*
Kirkuk, *33*
Kish, 41-2, 44, 63
Kurlil, *44*

Lagash, 41, 60, 65, 67-8; *3, 35, 72*
Lamma, *88*
Larsa, 78, 86; *86*
Lipit Ishtar, *81*
Lugal-zage-si, 61-2

Magan, *65*
Maghzaliya, 16-17
Mandali, *41*

Mari, 50, 71, 79, 84, 86
Mediterranean 20, 62, 67, 77, 79; *62*
Moon god, 47; *65, 75*
Moses, 63

Nanna, 47
Naram-Sin, 65, 67; *65, 69*
Neolithic revolution, 14-15
Nineveh, 19, 84; *23, 37, 46*
Ninevite 5 period/culture, 49; *46*
Ninhursag, *11, 43, 45*
Nippur, 44, 50, 65, 84-5
Noah, 40

Old Babylonian culture/period, 74-87
Oman, 34, 58; *26, 65*

Pacific, 19
Pu-abi, *52, 54, 58, 59*
Pythagoras, 81

Rim-Sin, *86*
Rome, Romans, 6

Samarra period/culture, 19, 28; *13*
Samsuiluna, 84-5
Sargon, 61-4, 87
Shamshi-Adad, 79-80
Shulgi, 70, 87; *65, 76*
Sin, 47
Sippar, *40, 94*
Standard of Ur, *5, 10, 36, 51*
Sumer(ian), 35, 40-73, 84
Sun god, 67
Syria, 6, 19-20, 50, 62; *85*

Tell al-Rimah, *37*
Tell al-'Ubaid, 18, 24; *11, 18, 43, 44, 45, 96*
Tell as-Sawwan, 17

Tell Brak, *25, 28, 29*
Tell Halaf, 18, 24
Tell Hammam, *73*
Tell Hassuna, 18
Tell Taya, 45, 71; *42, 80*
Tepe Gawra, 27-8
Third Dynasty of Ur, 69-78, 84
Tigris, 6, 10, 13, 19-20, 25, 39, 41; *2*
Turkey, 6, 16, 20, 27-8, 58, 62, 77, 86; *12*

Ubaid period/culture, 24-8, 30, 35; *18, 20, 22,*
Umm Dabaghiya, 17
Umma, 41, 60-1; *73*
Ur, 47, 50, 54, 58, 59, 69-71, 73, 77, 84; *5-6, 8, 10, 20, 22, 32, 36-7, 48, 50-63, 65, 74-8, 81, 84, 87-91*
Urkish, 71
Ur-Nammu, 69-70, 74; *75, 82, 86*

Ur-Ningirsu, *72*
Uru-inim-gina, 61, 74; *3*
Uruk, 29-31, 34-5, 36, 42, 44, 50, 68, 82, 84; *9, 21, 29, 44, 86*
Uruk period/culture, 29-31, 34-5; *9, 21, 80*
Utu-hegal, 68